Also by Lisa Jardine

A Point of View

Going Dutch: How England Plundered Holland's Glory

The Awful End of Prince William the Silent

The Curious Life of Robert Hooke:
The Man Who Measured London

On a Grander Scale: The Outstanding Career of
Sir Christopher Wren

Ingenious Pursuits: Building the Scientific Revolution

Wordly Goods: A New History of the Renaissance

Reading Shakespeare Historically

Erasmus, Man of Letters:
The Construction of Charisma in Print

Still Harping on Daughters

Francis Bacon: Discovery and the Art of Discourse

ANOTHER POINT OF VIEW

Lisa Jardine

Drawings by Nick Wadley

preface

Published by Preface 2009

10 9 8 7 6 5 4 3 2 1

Copyright © Lisa Jardine 2009
Drawings © Nick Wadley 2009

Lisa Jardine has asserted her right to be identified as the author of this work under the
Copyright, Designs and Patents Act 1988

Nick Wadley has asserted his right to be identified as the illustrator of this work under the
Copyright, Designs and Patents Act 1988

First published in Great Britain in 2009 by Preface Publishing
1 Queen Anne's Gate
London SW1H 9BT

An imprint of The Random House Group Limited

www.rbooks.co.uk
www.prefacepublishing.co.uk

Addresses for companies within The Random House Group Limited
can be found at www.randomhouse.co.uk

The Random House Group Limited Reg. No. 954009

A CIP catalogue record for this book is available from the British Library

ISBN 978 1 84809 099 6

The Random House Group Limited supports The Forest Stewardship
Council (FSC), the leading international forest certification organisation.
All our titles that are printed on Greenpeace-approved FSC-certified paper
carry the FSC logo. Our paper procurement policy can be found at
www.rbooks.co.uk/environment

Typeset by Palimpsest Book Production Limited, Grangemouth, Stirlingshire

Printed and bound in Great Britain by CPI Bookmarque, Croydon CR0 4TD

For John

Introduction

Since my first published collection of *A Point of View* talks on BBC Radio 4 appeared in 2008, the Sunday morning slot these broadcasts occupy, and which was previously the home of Alistair Cooke's *Letter from America*, has established itself yet more securely in the weekly broadcasting schedule. It has become the place where a number of highly-regarded, independent-minded and thoughtful individuals give spirited expression to their considered personal views on almost any subject you can think of. I particularly enjoy sharing the slot with veteran writer and broadcaster Clive James, whose engaging essays are always guaranteed to make me think and smile at the same time. Our contributions could not, I think, be more different. In fact, the title of this book — *Another Point of View* – captures something of that distinctiveness. Yet we both evidence a passionate desire to share our thoughts on whatever issue has taken our attention, and triggered our excitement, with a wider audience.

I still wish that, like Alistair Cooke, we were allowed to begin the Friday transmission of our talks with a courteous 'good evening', to be replaced on Sunday morning with an equally warm 'good morning'. These broadcasts feel very much like a conversation with the gratifyingly many listeners, and I treasure their intimacy. Equally, it would be nice to be able to sign off with something as comfortingly familiar as his regular: 'goodnight'. But times, I suppose, have changed, and broadcasters are no longer expected to observe such courtesies.

Each talk is supposed to take as its starting point something that has happened in the preceding week which has caught one's attention, and triggered a particular train of thought. This means that when preparing my Points of View I find myself more than usually sensitive to what is going on in the world around me. The period covered by these essays has been an especially turbulent one. Climate change and the behaviour of banks and stock markets have been consistent themes, and generated regular news stories. In spite of the apparent modernity of both these 'crises', I have tried in my reflections upon them to do justice to the very considerable amount of history (and thus valuable experience) that lies behind them. As always, I am committed to the view that the more we understand about comparable events in the past, the better we are likely to be able to understand the present, and the more reliably and purposefully plan for the future.

So the texts of these talks are offered in the spirit of openness and collaboration, to encourage anyone who cares to read them to continue the thought-processes begun here. Many of you have already done so, in letters, emails and posts on the BBC website, composed immediately after the first transmission of a particular programme. My friends and colleagues have waylaid me in corridors and at dinner tables to challenge me on specific points Much of what you have all had to say has fascinated me, and often led me to return to a subject with which I thought I had finished, to take it up again and to take its argument further.

I single out one person who has added significantly to the impact of my radio talks as they have moved from voice to print. Nick Wadley has provided his own comment in the form of an often wry illustration, adding to the impact of each piece with his keen eye and sharp wit. I think I knew the very first time that I spotted an illustration of his, and asked if he would be prepared to be my illustrator, that ours would be a fruitful and enjoyable partnership.

To all of those, then, who have participated in this shared endeavour – whether supportively or critically – I offer my thanks. I look forward to many more sharp encounters with the listening public in the future.

Lisa Jardine
December 2008

3

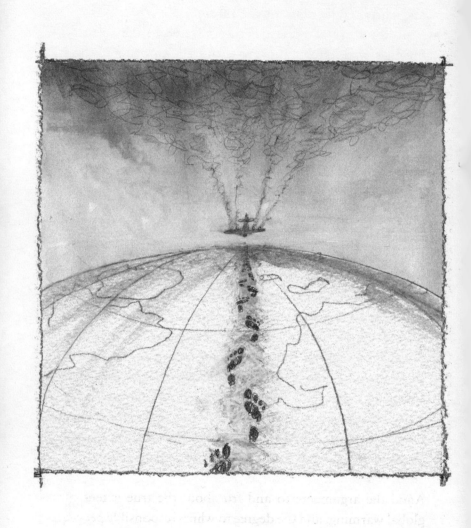

One

In September 2007, satellite images revealed that the Northwest Passage – the fabled, long sought-for northern sea-route connecting the Atlantic to the Pacific oceans, and thus Europe to Asia – was free of ice for the first time since records began. I wondered whether we should greet this news with delight, in the name of the fearless early navigators who lost their lives in those Arctic wastes, or whether this should be treated as one more grave warning of the damage we are doing to our planet.

Amid the arguments to and fro about the true extent of global warming, and the degree to which responsible people ought to be alarmed, I find one recent piece of news of the consequences of climate change particularly arresting.

Warming temperatures are melting the Arctic sea ice, making hitherto inaccessible stretches of the Arctic Ocean fully navigable. This September, satellite images showed the Northwest Passage to be ice free for the first time since records began, allowing shipping to travel comparatively unhindered from the Atlantic to the Pacific Ocean.

For more than five hundred years, since Columbus first encountered the continent of America, European mariners have dreamed of finding and navigating a Northwest Passage – a direct shipping route from Europe to Asia across the Arctic Ocean. It ought surely to be possible, they argued, to sail from European ports northwards along the coast of Greenland, then westwards along an Arctic parallel, round Baffin Island off the northern coast of Canada, entering the Pacific between Alaska and Russia?

The search, in the sixteenth century, for a corridor between the frozen northern wastes and the treacherous ice floes was driven by intense international competition and commercial pressures. Indeed, without the promise of financial gain riding on the outcome of these costly expeditions there would have been no financial backers. The existing sea-route eastwards round the Cape of Good Hope, to India, China and the Spice Islands with their rich resources of pepper, cinnamon and nutmeg, was long and dangerous. If a way could be found from the Atlantic Ocean into the Pacific which stayed close to the North Pole, the new class of entrepreneurial merchants would be able to undercut their rivals by having their sea-captains bring their exotic cargoes home faster and more economically.

In 1566, in his *Discourse of a Discoverie for a new Passage to Cataia [China],* the English mariner Sir Humphrey Gilbert urged Queen Elizabeth I to support the search for the Northwest Passage in terms which still resonate today:

'It were the only way for our princes to possess the wealth of all the east parts (as they term them) of the world, which is infinite . . . For, through the shortness of the voyage, we should be able to sell all manner of merchandise brought from thence far better cheap than either the Portuguese or Spaniard doth or may do.'

Eye-witness accounts survive of several of the early failed attempts to find a navigable way round (or through) the new continent. The sailors who limped home on their battered and broken ships, convey with shocking vividness the punishing effects of the extreme cold and the treacherously mobile ice floes, the relentlessly destructive effects of hunger and exhaustion. Whole expeditions perished, some of their bodies discovered many years later, frozen and intact in the hulls of their ships.

These early explorers never succeeded in finding their shortcut. But in the process of failing to reach their El Dorado, they stumbled upon other, hitherto unknown territories, which turned out to be of equivalent, if not greater importance for success in a newly global economy.

The English mariner Henry Hudson made four attempts at finding a passage through Arctic waters between 1607 and 1611. His determination to prove that such a route existed bordered on the obsessive. On the final attempt, both he and his son John perished, set adrift in an open

boat by their mutinous crew, who balked at the prospect
of another prolonged period of fruitlessly negotiating the
never-ending frozen wastes in the region subsequently
named Hudson Bay.

For his first two attempts, Hudson sailed due north from
England, then turned eastwards to try to skirt the northern
coast of Russia. Almost locked in to a frozen sea off the
island of Nova Zembla, he was forced to turn back, and
his backers abandoned him. Undeterred, Hudson found a
new investor in the form of the Dutch East India Company,
and set off again in the summer of 1609 on his ship the
Half Moon.

It was this third voyage that accidentally proved his most
successful. Hudson had determined views on routes and
agendas. Although his Dutch contract committed him to
pursuing the eastwards route around the Pole he had
attempted before, faced once more with extreme cold and
floating ice, Hudson impetuously decided to abandon this
shortly after embarkation. Instead he headed westwards
towards North America, to take up a suggestion of Captain
John Smith's (the first Governor of Virginia) that a northerly
navigable river might lead across the continent, and out
the other side to the Spice Islands.

On 12 September 1609, the *Half Moon* entered the
mouth of what is now called the Hudson River – 'as fine
a river as can be found, wide and deep, with good anchoring
ground on both sides', 'a very good harbour for all winds',
according to a contemporary account. The land around
was 'very pleasant and high'.

They were in the outer reaches of what today is New York harbour, riding along the coast of Staten Island. Fish swam around them in shoals. When they anchored and went ashore, they found 'friendly and polite people, who had an abundance of provisions, skins, and furs, of martens and foxes, and many other commodities, as birds and fruit, even white and red grapes, and they traded amicably with the people.' But sailing up the broad river as far as what is today Albany, the water became 'sweet' (not salty) and too shallow for a seagoing ship to pass. So this was not the route Hudson was looking for.

But on Hudson's return, his Dutch backers quickly recognised that the area of the New World Hudson had explored was worth further exploration and exploitation. The history of the Dutch colony of New Amsterdam on Manhattan Island (famously acquired in 1626 from the Indian tribe that lived there for goods to the value of 60 guilders) is a rich one in its own right. Had that pivotal North American colony not been seized by the British 38 years later, the entire western world might today be speaking Dutch.

The search for the Northwest Passage continued down to the nineteenth century. In 1845, Sir John Franklin with two ships and a crew of more than 120 men disappeared without trace in the Arctic wastes. By that time the commercial world was beginning to direct its efforts to improve long distance trade routes elsewhere, leading eventually to the building of the Suez Canal in 1869 and the Panama Canal in 1914.

Today our relentless search for essential natural resources, given added urgency by our profligate consumption of gas and oil, has reopened international interest in accessing that elusive Northwest Passage. For now the research scientists exploring the region – the last areas on earth to be fully explored – insist that their endeavours are concentrated on understanding climate change and global warming for the good of humankind.

But already governments have their eye on long-term possibilities for control of our ever-depleting stocks of oil and gas. In the Arctic, Canada and the United States are at loggerheads over who controls the freezing waters of the Northwest Passage, while Russia claims to be entitled to exploit the natural resources underneath the North Pole.

Meanwhile, in the southern hemisphere, the tenacious hold Britain has maintained on the islands of South Georgia and the Falklands, which resulted twenty years ago in our going to war with Argentina over the sovereignty of those two remote and windswept pieces of land, finally begins to make sense to me. The pursuit of British polar interests in the twenty-first century may owe more to Margaret Thatcher than we realise.

That sovereignty supports Britain's claim to territorial rights over a sweeping arc of the Antarctic Ocean under which may lie those priceless natural resources – resources also claimed vociferously by Argentina and Chile. Twelve other nations, including Australia, New Zealand, Russia, and by historical adventure, Norway and Japan, make more measured claims, through peaceful cooperation, enshrined in the 1961 Antarctic Treaty.

Is it too late to find a way to preserve the altruistic tone of scientific collaboration that these inhospitable and remote regions have up to now enjoyed? Might we indeed go further – could the nations of the world combine in their battle against global warming and succeed in reversing its tide, so that the Northwest Passage may once again become frozen and impassable?

Two

A visit to a retrospective exhibition of the work of the extraordinary French artist Louise Bourgeois (now in her 90s), on a grand scale, at Tate Modern in November 2007 brought home to me the sheer power of her creative imagination. It also led me to reflect on the role of museums in our twenty-first century world.

Ever since Louise Bourgeois's 30 foot high, menacing bronze sculptural spider first appeared at the opening of Tate Modern in London in 1999 – magnificently answering the challenge of how artists would address the cavernous space of the Turbine Hall in the heart of the reclaimed Bankside Power Station – I have wanted to know more about this powerful and prolific woman sculptor. Although her mature artistic career covered exactly the period in which I was growing up and being introduced to contemporary art by my artist mother, I had somehow heard very little about her.

I was apparently not alone. This autumn, Tate Modern is giving us the chance to see a full range of Louise Bourgeois works in a dizzyingly wide range of media, created over a period of almost seventy years (she is 95 years old, and still working), in a major retrospective exhibition covering 11,000 square feet of the gallery.

And the monumental spider is back – 'Maman' [Mummy] as she is titled, her motherhood visible in the gleaming white, oversized marble eggs, suspended in a steel mesh sac under her giant abdomen. This time she broods splendidly over the paved area outside the Thames-side entrance to the gallery, her finely arched, segmented legs like the vaulting of a cathedral over your head. If you stand with your back to the gallery and look across the river, she frames (and appears to dwarf) the dome of St Paul's.

Working in media from latex, stitched fabric and painted wood, to bronze, marble and steel, on a scale from the minute to the grandiose, Bourgeois's work reflects repeatedly upon incidents of crisis from her own emotional life – from the fraught anguish of childhood betrayal (her father's long-running affair with her own governess) to the complex states of mind engendered by the conflicting demands of a creative and a domestic life. She is an artist who requires that we respond to her art with a passion to match her own.

Last weekend, as dusk fell, my husband and I set off to take a tour of the exhibition, in the evening hours after 6 which modern museums now offer as an opportunity for working Londoners to spend calm leisure time in their spectacular interiors. We find these late-night openings magical, with their heady mix of unhurried intellectual opportunity and friendly social interaction. There is always something of a party atmosphere as you mingle with your fellow visitors, scrutinize and occasionally chat to the intriguing mix of other twilight museum-goers – many young couples, a few families, quite a number of gregarious groups of teenagers, and of course, older people like ourselves who have chosen this alternative to a Saturday evening in front of the television. As everywhere in London, English is the language of interaction, but only one of the many lilting languages to be overheard in snippets as you move back and forth between exhibits.

The idea of a museum visit as a kind of promenade theatre event is a comparatively new one for me. I am typical of my generation, I suspect, in still expecting a trip to a gallery to be improving – with the emphasis on it as a place where one will be educated, and above all, somewhere where one will be infused with morally uplifting sentiments. Younger gallery-goers, by contrast, go in search of a more immediate experience – looking for something emotionally challenging, against which to measure the tide of undigested information that floods us, in our engulfing sea of online information. Or, in the case of Tate Modern's Turbine Hall or the V&A's Friday Late, they simply go to hang out with similarly inclined others, for the shared sense of occasion.

In fact, last weekend's outing to Tate Modern succeeded in convincing me that the excitement of the encounter is an important part of today's visit to the museum. On Saturday night we entered the gallery to find that the vast concrete slab floor of the Turbine Hall had been fractured by a 584 ft [167 m] long fault-line – a jagged, zig-zagging crack, varying along its length in width and depth, extending from a single point at the top of the entrance ramp, as if the building had been struck by an earthquake, or with a giant pick-axe.

This is the much talked-about 'Shibboleth', by the Colombian artist Doris Salcedo, a work intended to shift our perception of the world we live in, to remind us that the monumentality and grandeur of the gallery's architecture is undermined by the history of discrimination and tension between peoples that lies beneath the surface of modernity. A 'shibboleth' is a custom, or idiomatic phrase, used as a test, to check who belongs to a particular ethnic or social group, and to exclude those who 'don't belong'. 'Shibboleth represents borders, the experience of segregation', says Salcedo. 'So this piece is a negative space'.

The juxtaposition of 'Shibboleth' with Louise Bourgeois's intensely personal art made me stop and think about the nature and purpose of cultural spaces in our modern world. What do we want nowadays, when we enter a gallery or museum?

According to the French public intellectual André

Malraux – Minister for Culture under General de Gaulle for ten years (from 1959–69) – whereas once the visitor went to a museum to be provided with answers, now the responsibility lies with us, the visitors. The museum experience exists most richly and vividly in our own imaginations – created out of a collection of images we each carry with us, gleaned from books, magazines, photographs and film. We bring remembered visual material with us into a museum space which has thereby become 'imaginary'. The installation or exhibition merely acts as a catalyst, prompting us to ask our own questions which we look to the artist to answer. 'Modern museums have imposed on the viewer an absolutely new relationship with respect to the work of art,' wrote Malraux. 'The museum was once an affirmation, the Imaginary Museum is an interrogation'.

As if to provide a perfect example of Malraux's visitor-directed museum experience, those roaming up and down the Turbine Hall last weekend seemed to be making their own meaning, rather than following an itinerary mapped out by the artist. Hands were held across the crack at its widest points, children stood arms akimbo over it peering downwards, groups clustered as if in consultation at the points where it deepened, or changed direction. Everyone was taking photographs on their mobile phone. It was as if they wanted to heal that negative, scarring fracture.

Cultural spaces like Tate Modern can give purpose and a sense of direction to hectic modern lives. We want to get close to and understand artists with their powerful, concretely realised explanations of human experience. Crucially, we seem to want to do this in a communal place – meeting, sharing and reinforcing our moments of understanding.

It has become something of a truism nowadays to describe the museum as a modern, secular cathedral – something already proposed in William Hazlitt's early nineteenth-century characterisation of the National Gallery in London as 'a sanctuary, holy of holies, collected by taste, sacred to fame, enriched by the rarest products of genius'.

But the twenty-first century gallery-goer, I suggest, no longer wishes to be awed by the completeness of the collection, or lectured on the importance of a particular theme. Those meticulously structured, organised and labelled specialist exhibitions which seem most explicitly designed to be instructive may well be experienced by the modern visitor as controlling and coercive. They seem to deny the individual access on their own terms, to leave them no room to breathe. The expert curators self-consciously hold them at arm's length from the project – talking amongst themselves, and withholding approval unless the visitor is prepared to follow a pre-arranged route to a predetermined goal.

The Imaginary Museum, on the other hand, lays itself open to creatively kaleidoscope acts of engagement on the part of those who enter it. It welcomes, and finds a place for the unexpected collisions that may occur between the visitor's prior knowledge and experience and the objects on display. The visitor, meanwhile, feels challenged to use their own initiative and accumulated experience to make sense of what is laid out enticingly before them. Which is certainly what happened to me last weekend at the Tate.

Three

When, in autumn 2007, the clocks went forward in the United States several weeks earlier than in Europe, ostensibly as part of an energy saving drive on the part of the Republican administration in the US, it disturbed my weekly routine of calling my elderly mother in California from my home in London at the same time every Sunday evening. This is not the first time that politics has interfered with the clocks, and I was led to reflect on some earlier, significant occasions on which time difference played its part in shaping history.

For the past forty years, my mother – now ninety – has lived in California. These days we try to talk to one another on the telephone several times a week, in the middle of the morning her time, which – eight hours on – is the end of my working day.

Last week the reassuring routineness of our regular calls suffered a small but significant confusion. The United States, without any particular fanfare, put its clocks forward three weeks earlier than those of the European Union, on the second Sunday in March, and put them back a week late last Sunday – on the first Sunday in November, rather than (as we did here) on the last Sunday in October. So when my mother phoned at her usual time, she found me only seven hours ahead of her, barely home from work, rather than comfortably settled in the living room awaiting her call.

These changes in dates for Daylight Saving Time are part of the Energy Policy Act, signed into law by President Bush in August 2005, which came into force this year. And there were political motives behind President Bush's tinkering with the clocks.

The Energy Policy Act is a set of measures ostensibly aimed at reducing America's emission of greenhouse gases, and countering global warming – a set of what to me at least seem like token gestures on the part of the American Administration, to make up for their steadfast refusal to sign up to the Kyoto Protocol with its targets for industrialised countries to cut their greenhouse gas emissions. Increasing Daylight Saving Time supposedly makes a significant contribution to energy conservation.

It was rumoured, too, that the extension of Daylight Saving Time beyond the end of October came in response to lobbying by the American confectionery industry. Sweet manufacturers wanted a Daylight Saving Time extension so that the clocks were turned back after Hallowe'en. The extra hour of daylight on 31 October would mean more time when parents could safely let their children go 'trick-or-treating', with resulting enhanced sales for the basketfuls of 'candy' traditionally handed out to them.

The most overtly political aspect of the Energy Policy Act, though, is that in its entirety it has so little regard for its impact on the rest of the world. Its measures were introduced with scant evidence of consultation outside the United States. Yet several of them – including the alteration of Daylight Saving Time – have had knock-on effects beyond North America.

The Act offers tax incentives to American farmers to change from growing grain for human consumption, to planting maize, sugar cane, palm oil and oil seed rape instead, all of which can be turned into biofuels. Tax incentives are also offered to fuel providers, if they can offer higher percentages of clean fuels on the filling-station forecourt. But the altered pattern of crop-growing produced by this US legislation – enthusiastically embraced by rural farmers – has already helped drive up the price of bread in Britain, pasta in Italy and tortillas in Mexico.

We tend to think of time as tethered to the seasons and governed by the inexorable movement of the planets. Yet in spite of the fact that we behave, in general, as if the variations of clocks, time and time zones were natural and inevitable, politicians have tampered with time on many occasions in the past.

The idea of Daylight Saving Time itself was only seriously proposed in Britain exactly a century ago, as a politically acceptable means of extending the working day. William Willett, a keen early-morning horseman, noticed as he rode near his home early on a summer's morning, how many of the local residents were still asleep. In 1907 he published a pamphlet entitled 'The Waste of Daylight', in which he pointed out how many more hours could be got out of labourers if clocks went forward in summer time. Summer time as we know it was introduced in 1916.

In October 1582, it was politics that decided the English not to follow suit, when Catholic Europe complied with a papal edict decreeing that ten days be removed from the calendar to bring it back in line with that in use in AD 325, at the time of the first Council of Nicaea, thereby helping the vexed question of how to calculate the date of Easter. Across Catholic Europe that year, 4 October was followed by 15 October, apparently without much fuss. But in spite of the fact that the learned English mathematician Dr John Dee counselled that calendar reform was essential, Queen Elizabeth I's Protestant administration chose not to comply.

It was not until 1752 that the English calendar (and that of her American colonies) was finally brought into line with that of the rest of Europe. By then the change necessitated the removal of eleven days – to account for the fact that the new calendar, but not the old, made 1700 a leap-year. When Wednesday 2 September 1752 was followed by Thursday 14 September, there was rioting on the streets of London – vividly captured in a painting by William

Hogarth, in which the angry mob carries a banner with the slogan 'Give us our eleven days'.

In fact, recent research has established that the change produced no widespread unrest. But it did cause social and economic confusion. In spite of assurances to the contrary, labourers lost eleven days' pay, and many annual contracts were adjusted downwards financially to take account of the shortened period. The King (George II) chose to move his birthday from 11 to 22 June, so as not to shorten the length of his reign.

And to ensure consistency of financial record-keeping, the official English fiscal year was never shortened, with the result that in the United Kingdom alone, the tax year begins on a uniquely odd date. Add 11 days to the traditional 25 March start to the financial year and you get to 6 April – which has been the beginning of our tax year ever since.

My favourite calendar-driven piece of political finessing is less well known, though hardly less historically significant.

In late autumn 1688, the Protestant ruler of the Netherlands, William of Orange, embarked from the naval port of Hellevoetsluis, to invade England and claim the throne on behalf of himself and his wife Mary, the reigning Catholic King James II's eldest daughter. His invasion force consisted of an astounding five hundred ships, an army of more than twenty thousand highly trained professional troops, and a further twenty thousand mariners and support staff.

The vast Dutch fleet was swept by a 'providential wind' along the south coast of England, miraculously avoiding the English fleet in the Thames estuary, arriving off Torbay on 3 November – or rather, on what William's advisors considered to be 13 November, since they, along with the rest of Continental Europe (but not England), used the 'new' Gregorian calendar. William of Orange's birthday was on 14 November. Many in his entourage urged him to take advantage of the significance of that day to launch his invasion. Such a landing date would, they argued, strike the English as propitious.

But as far as the English were concerned, the date on which William's birthday fell was still ten days away. So Prince William and his fleet decided to lay off the English coast just two more days before landing, commencing disembarkation on what according to the English calendar was 5 November 1688 – known today as Guy Fawkes Day.

Thus it was that the landing which began the so-called 'Glorious Revolution' took place on the anniversary of another great triumph of English Protestantism over the hostile forces of Catholicism – the uncovering of the Gunpowder Plot in 1605. The convenient match with the familiar date meant that Catholic threats were uppermost in Englishmen's minds. The annual bonfires lit across the country to celebrate James I's narrow escape from a terrorist plot, announced the arrival of the man who would drive the Catholic King James II from the throne of England.

So whenever politicians turn their attention to calendars and clocks, we should take a long hard look beyond the apparently innocuous practical benefits proposed. There is bound to be something more considerable at stake than an extra hour in bed.

September 1752

Sun	Mon	Tues	Wed	Thur	Fri	Sat
*	*	1	2	~~3~~	~~4~~	~~5~~
~~6~~	~~7~~	~~8~~ (Sat)	~~9~~ (Sun)	~~10~~ (Mon)	~~11~~ (Tues)	~~12~~
~~13~~ (Wed)	14 (thurs)	15 (Fri)	16	17	18	19
20	21	22	23	24	25	26
27	28	29	30	*	*	*

Four

For the academic year 2007–8 I was seconded to the Royal Society in London, as advisor to their magnificent collections of manuscripts and documents, dating back to the foundation of this great scientific institution in the 1660s. While leafing through a handwritten copy of Sir Isaac Newton's Principia *which he had himself annotated and corrected, I came upon a marginal note in his handwriting in which he registered the arrival on the English throne in 1685 of the Catholic king, James II, For a moment I hoped that I might be about to get behind the mask of the mathematician to the innermost feelings of the man himself.*

Is the urge to recover the inner life of great figures from the past a purely modern tendency, I wonder? I certainly find myself reflecting regularly upon how the author of a work I am reading might have felt at the time he or she was writing. The merest trace of emotion in a long-unread letter or a marginal note in a book produces a surge of excitement, as I try to reconstruct their original state of mind.

Here's one that happened to me this week. Among the treasures to be found in the Library of the Royal Society in London (where I currently work), is a handwritten copy of Sir Isaac Newton's groundbreaking work, the *Principia*, with Newton's own marginal corrections, along with additional calculations and further annotations added on facing pages. In the *Principia* – or to give it its full name in English, the *Mathematical Principles of Natural Philosophy* – Newton brilliantly laid out in mathematical terms the principles of time, force and motion that have underpinned developments in the modern physical sciences ever since, at least until Einstein's theory of relativity further refined the picture. It is a work of mathematical and conceptual virtuosity which, however, reveals little about the man behind the ideas.

Last Monday, however, as I was leafing through the Royal Society's manuscript *Principia* I noticed for the first time a doodle by Newton in the section on 'the motion of bodies in moveable orbits'. Upside down on a blank page he had scribbled in English, 'James the 2d by the grease [grace] of god King of . . .' My heart leapt when I saw it.

What had been Newton's state of mind as he wrote those words? He was correcting his manuscript less than a year after the unexpected death of Charles II from complications brought on by a stroke, and the hasty Coronation of his brother James II. Newton, like many of his devoutly Protestant contemporaries, deeply disapproved of James's Catholic beliefs and practices, yet the *Principia* when published in 1687 would carry a title page celebrating him as reigning monarch. Might I have discovered evidence that the great mathematician was worrying about his future and the future of his country, as he wrestled with the final details of his three laws of motion, and perfected the theory of gravitational attraction?

Alas, comb the pages as I might, there were no further clues to be found anywhere else in the volume. Nor did contemporary letters from Newton to his devoted editor Edmund Halley, also preserved in the Royal Society strongroom, shed any further light on the matter. As is so often the case, the paper trail of historical evidence simply ran out.

I think it must be this thirst for the 'real life' sentiments of the person behind the celebrity that makes me a serious fan of romantic Hollywood movies about English history. When Bette Davis slaps Errol Flynn's face in the 1939 classic, *The Private Lives of Elizabeth and Essex* ('You dare turn your back on Elizabeth of England, you dare?') the historian in me is prepared to overlook the glaring anachronisms in the film simply because the screen version allows me genuinely to feel a surge of pride for the Virgin Queen.

And I confess the same was true last week when I saw the historical movie of the moment, Shekhar Kapur's *Elizabeth: The Golden Age*. In this latest glorious celebration of one of history's great iconic women, Cate Blanchett reprises her widely-acclaimed 1998 role as Queen Elizabeth I, Geoffrey Rush is once again the passionately loyal, if ruthless, Sir Francis Walsingham, while Clive Owen plays a gallantly seductive Sir Walter Raleigh – Errol Flynn-style.

Critical reception of *Elizabeth: The Golden Age* in the British media has not matched the chorus of approval from American critics. There have been murmurings of reproach over the film's breaches in historical authenticity, with commentators expressing their anxiety at its tampering with the facts, and the liberties taken with the plot, in terms of what can only be described as moral dismay. Ought I as an historian to share the critics' disapproval? The fact is, I simply don't.

Because after a career spent poring over the surviving documents from the sixteenth and seventeenth centuries, clutching at any emotional straw in the form of an over-looked manuscript jotting or a recently-discovered folio of contemporary eye-witness observations, I find the heroic confidence of Blanchett's portrayal of Elizabeth I positively exhilarating.

Magnificently decked out in breathtaking outfits, topped by a sequence of elaborately eye-catching hairstyles, her reposte to the Spanish Ambassador's threat to send an Armada against our little islands has the ring of Joan of Arc about it: 'I too can command the wind, Sir! I have a hurricane in me that will strip Spain bare if you dare to try me!' And on her rearing white horse in a glittering suit of armour, she is Henry V at the siege of Honfleur (or at least Kenneth Branagh's version of him in his remake of

Laurence Olivier's classic film), as she urges on her troops:
'Let them come with the armies of hell, they will not pass!'

The skill of the film director lies in introducing the
emotional texture and pulse of history by means of vivid
tableaux and screen images, to prompt in us the rush of
feeling I have just described. In *Elizabeth: the Golden Age*,
Shekhar Kapur – a former Bollywood director – deliber-
ately recapitulates the over-heated encounters between Bette
Davis and Errol Flynn in *The Private Lives of Elizabeth
and Essex*, just as he does that iconic moment on a rearing
white horse in Shakespeare's *Henry V*.

Indeed, consider the way in which William Shakespeare
himself heightened the emotional atmosphere in his play,
to allow an anxious England – worrying about the succes-
sion as their unmarried, childless queen grew old – to
conjure up the glory days of her forbear Henry V and find
reassurance. The romantic courtship between Henry and
the French Princess Katherine in the play substitutes for a
more prosaic reality – Henry actually won his bride as
spoils of war. And does the documentary record tell us
that Henry really uttered the words, 'Once more unto the
breach, dear friends, once more; / Or close the wall up
with our English dead'? Of course not.

Yet these are the ringing words which, time and again,
have been used to engender in the British the strong emotions
of national pride which we associate with key moments in
our real or imagined history. I remember being startled, in
1989, when, listening to the 5 p.m. news on my car radio,
I heard the then Chairman of the Conservative Party,

Kenneth Baker, at the Party Conference, urging the party faithful to stiffen their resolve in the face of a proposed increase in mortgage lending rates, to extraordinary rhetorical effect: 'And in the words of Henry V at Agincourt – "He that hath no stomach for the fight / Let him depart ...'". The rest of Baker's speech was drowned in an emotional roar of audience approval.

To censure the efforts of generations of screen-writers and movie directors because they fail to stick to the truth is, in my opinion, to miss the point. Where they succeed, as in my view *Elizabeth: the Golden Age* does, they tap into that yearning I have described in myself. They allow us to connect the events of the past with the threads of emotion and feeling which make that past meaningful for us in the present. They rediscover, in a way the documents generally cannot, the humanity of those who were agents of our history.

We might reflect, too, that *Elizabeth: the Golden Age* is a movie by an Indian director, with an Australian star, from a British studio and an American distributor. How extraordinary that around the world there should be enough fascination with this quintessentially English story, to make a movie based upon it a box-office success.

The silver screen has once again exuberantly travestied a glorious moment in our history – as it has since talkies began. Rather than cavilling at the obvious elisions and anachronisms, ought we not self-confidently to revel in the universal appeal of the story of an underdog nation triumphing against the odds, and the creative retellings it continues to inspire?

Five

The Orpheus myth – in which the power of a lyre-player's music charms the gods into allowing him to retrieve his lost love Eurydice from the underworld – explores music's power to raise the human spirit above the mundane. It has been used repeatedly by composers and film-makers to explore the human yearning towards spirituality and access to the metaphysical and divine. As I prepared to attend a conference celebrating the 400th anniversary year of the first performance of Claudio Monteverdi's opera L'Orfeo, I reflected on the perennial power of music to move us.

It is 400 years since the first performance, on 24 February 1607, in the presence of the Gonzaga Duke of Mantua, Vincenzo I, of the seventeenth-century Italian composer

Claudio Monteverdi's opera *L'Orfeo* [Orpheus]. This weekend I am attending a three-day international symposium at the University of Leeds to mark that anniversary.

L'Orfeo is considered by many to be the earliest 'real' opera, and the Orpheus myth on which it is based has permeated art and music since antiquity. The story – found in Virgil, Horace and Ovid – has inspired operas by Monteverdi, Gluck, Offenbach and Philip Glass, plays by Tennessee Williams and Jean Anouilh, and evocative paintings by artists from Pieter Paul Rubens to Marc Chagall. One of my own favourite reworkings of the theme is the 1959 Oscar-winning film, *Black Orpheus* [Orfeu Negro], by the French director Marcel Camus, set in Rio during Carnival, suffused throughout by the insistent rhythms of samba.

The theme all works of art based on the Orpheus myth explore in their various ways is music's quasi-divine power to raise the human spirit above the mundane, crossing boundaries, and breaking down taboos. Since mankind inhabited the earth, every society has had its own rituals to establish who is acceptable to the community and who is not.

Nowadays we are, I think, more conscious than ever before that the sharp boundaries between acceptable and unacceptable beliefs and practices vary widely from culture to culture. The 'good manners' many of us cherish may turn out to be out of place in the company of strangers. The lines of demarcation between behaviour those in any particular country consider to be 'polite' and 'impolite', sometimes turn out to be strikingly different from those in the one with which we are most familiar.

On my last visit to Japan, I ventured into a large 'Departo' or department store in Osaka. Having collected together an armful of garments to try on in the womens-wear department, I was gestured with smiles and bows towards a run of curtained changing booths at the back of the section, which stood on a kind of raised plinth. As I drew back the curtain and prepared to step in, I was stopped short by an aghast chorus of shrieks from behind me. It was as well I paused and took notice. In Japan, it turns out, you do not enter a department-store changing room without removing your shoes. In their eyes, I had been on the point of polluting a pristinely 'clean' space, by my breach of Japanese manners.

It was the great anthropologist Mary Douglas – one of my own intellectual heroes, who, sadly, died earlier this year – who famously made the observation that what any society designates as 'dirt' is not fundamentally a category of material polluted by germs or microbes, but is a case of 'matter out of place'. In her classic book, *Purity and Danger*, she described how every society surrounds itself with patterns and ordered classifications which give it a sustaining sense of order. In the world we inhabit, every-thing has its allotted place, and keeping it thus is what supposedly makes us civilised. If anything undesirable intrudes, or happens to disturb that order, the discordant element is recognised and dealt with by giving it the label 'dirty'.

So, according to Douglas, a towel draped over the edge of the bath may be 'clean', but it becomes 'dirty' if it is then left on the sofa in the sitting-room. Shoes are not dirty in themselves, but it is dirty to place them on the dining-table – that was clearly how my Japanese shop-assistants understood my almost entering their changing-room with my shoes on. In an undergraduate class of mine on Mary Douglas's work, an American exchange student observed that while the British consider that taking a bath is 'clean', those from the United States are appalled at the idea of wallowing in a bathful of one's own grubbiness. For her, taking a shower was 'clean', taking a bath was 'dirty'.

Mary Douglas was ultimately interested in rather more telling distinctions than those between clean and dirty bathwater. She wanted to understand how in different societies, different rituals separate the world of religion from the secular, everyday one. 'Dirt is matter out of place' was an idea she framed in order to explain the extraordinary range of ways in which different societies distinguish between what, in religious terms, is ritually 'pure' and what is 'defiling' or 'polluted'. Which comes down to the distinction between what is 'sacred' and what 'profane'.

In Douglas's terms, Jewish and Islamic food prohibitions, for example, reflect the two Abrahamic religions' historic desire to set their adherents apart from the members of the tribes around them. A systematic set of rules was put in place in relation to food (not eating pork products, not mixing meat and milk), non-compliance with which would automatically mean that an individual was labelled as 'unclean', and would be excluded. To breach the rule was to be 'unclean'. Because the rules are elaborate and quite complicated, they require considerable effort on the part of the observant, thereby binding members together to the exclusion of the non-observant, and making them subtly alert to infringements.

In context I find Douglas's argument pretty convincing. This past week, however, what has struck me is how compellingly music succeeds in blurring any distinction, however ritually clearly defined, between what belongs within the domains of the sacred and what within the secular.

It seems to have been acknowledged since antiquity that music has the capacity to move hearts and captivate the soul, so as to shade profane or secular delight into something like religious exultation. The myth of Orpheus and Eurydice beautifully captures this power of music to dissolve taboo boundaries, challenging the divide between profane and spiritual love, and ultimately even that between life and death.

The story goes, that Orpheus was the most accomplished musician in antiquity, the inventor of the lyre, whose exquisite playing could tame wild beasts, calm storms, and even divert the course of rivers. Distraught at the accidental death of his wife of a single day, Eurydice, his musical laments were so passionate that the gods themselves were moved to pity, and they agreed to allow him to descend into the underworld to find her. There his music melted the hearts of the gods of the underworld themselves, who consented to Eurydice's returning to the land of the living. There was one condition, however. Orpheus was to walk ahead of her, without looking back until they both reached the upper world. On the threshold, however, his human nature overcame him and he glanced behind him, before Eurydice had stepped back into the light. Immediately, she disappeared, separated from him for ever.

Music, the legend suggests, elevates the merely mundane to the realms of the divine, petitioning the gods with an urgency and directness that can overcome even the most powerful constraints on human effectiveness. Orpheus's love for Eurydice is profane, yet his poignant expression in music of his feelings at her loss persuades the gods to grant him his desire to redeem her from death.

It is fitting, then, that Monteverdi's *L'Orfeo* should be considered by historians of music as a kind of watershed at the beginning of the seventeenth century, between a European musical tradition whose ensemble performances were largely reserved for religious occasions, and the development of ambitious compositions for voice and orchestra to be performed on the secular stage – in particular, opera. Monteverdi's rich and glorious compositions cross effortlessly back and forth across that boundary. In the opening section of his 'Vespers for the Blessed Virgin', for instance, written in 1610, musical themes from *L'Orfeo* are reprised in a sacred composition for choir, soloists and orchestra.

Listening to Monteverdi's *L'Orfeo* and to the seductive samba rhythms from the soundtrack of the film, *Black Orpheus*, in preparation for my conference, I have found it hard to imagine that there is anyone who would not be moved by their harmonies. Together they sustain my personal conviction that there exist fundamental human values which make it possible to transcend local sectarianism and inter-factional conflict, to reach shared resolution. At a time of heightening global tensions, nationalist clamour and religious schism, the extraordinary power of music to unite its listeners gives me more than a glimmer of comfort.

Six

On a visit to Cambridge one crisp, clear evening in mid-November 2007, I discovered that the Christmas decorations were up and the festive lights already illuminated. It is easy to express disapproval and dismay at such a blatant example of seasonal enchantment combined with commercial opportunism. Yet throughout history, ostentatious expenditure has had its part to play in the celebration of the birth of Christ.

As I walked through the centre of Cambridge at the beginning of last week, just after dusk, the ancient streets which lead off the Market Square were decked out with a fairytale array of twinkling white lights and kaleidoscope-coloured Christmas ornaments. Rounding the bend in Rose

Crescent, I met a small boy and his father, coming towards me in the twilight, the child clutching his father's hand, his eyes bright with excitement, craning his neck to see the lights and decorations, and skipping with delight. 'But don't you think they are lovely?', he was saying, breathlessly. His father's answer was cautious – he clearly did not want to disappoint: 'Yes, I do think so. I just think it's a bit early'.

I have to confess here that, deep down, I was on the side of the little boy. I love the sense of expectation Christmas lights bring at the onset of the festive season – the sheer magic of the transformation they make.

I admit, though, that as far as the commercial hype and high-street shopping goes, Christmas seems to start earlier each year. The Christmas lights were switched on in London's Oxford Street this year on 7 November, the same date, actually, as last year, but a full week earlier than in 2005. This is early even by American standards – in the United States, where commercial interests are notoriously impatient to begin the 'festive' (or rather, holiday shopping) season, tradition until recently dictated that Christmas decorations in shops and streets were not put up till after Thanksgiving, on the last Thursday of November.

Tradition is a curious thing. It is remarkable how little time it takes for an attractive innovation – perhaps imported from another culture – to become 'traditional'.

Take the Christmas tree. Legend has it that Martin Luther began the tradition of decorating trees to celebrate

Christmas. One Christmas Eve in the late 1520s, so the story goes, he was walking through snow-covered woods and was struck by the beauty of a group of small fir trees, their branches, dusted with snow. When he got home, he set up a little tree indoors for his family, and decorated it with lighted candles. Whatever the substance in this story, the Christmas tree only caught on in Britain when the German prince Albert married the young Queen Victoria in 1840. Christmas trees became the rage after illustrated magazines published a picture of the royal couple and their children grouped around a table-top tree decorated with candles and glass ornaments.

And because the Christmas tree is only tangentially connected with the Christian Christmas story, it has become a shared festive symbol in cities around the world, and across faiths. In my own childhood home, the decking of the tree with my mother's treasure-trove collection of fragile glass ornaments was one of the high-points of our year, in spite of the fact that our background was Jewish.

'Father Christmas', or 'Santa Claus', such a familiar part of our children's Christmases, is another relatively new tradition. So distinctive is he as a seasonal figure, and so recognisable are his red jacket and trousers with their white edging, his red hat, curly white beard and big black boots, that it is hard to appreciate that in his current incarnation he dates back only to the twentieth century.

In Charles Dickens's day, Father Christmas – or the spirit of Christmas – wore dark green, and was garlanded in holly, making more obvious his relationship to the pagan figures from whom he is descended. Santa's red coat and white trim only became 'traditional' in the 1930s. An executive at Coca-Cola – whose logo was already the familiar red script on a white ground – noted the appropriateness of a depiction of a jolly white-bearded man in a red suit for seasonal advertising, and ran a series of ads featuring him.

There is a longer history of involvement than we might expect of buying and selling in creating some of the characteristic and comfortingly familiar symbols we associate with the celebration of Christmas.

Have you ever considered why, on countless Christmas cards, the figure of the Virgin Mary in a familiar Italian Renaissance painting – like the fifteenth-century Florentine painter Domenico Ghirlandaio's 'Adoration of the Magi', for instance – is invariably depicted dressed in a cloak or robe coloured the deepest blue?

Renaissance works of art were intended ostentatiously to advertise the power and wealth of the person or family who commissioned and paid for them. We are no longer attuned to the comparative expense of colour pigments. In the fifteenth-century, however, all paint hues were not perceived as equal, and the fifteenth-century viewer's eye would have registered the differences in colour and shade. Expanses of an expensive pigment indicated clearly the generosity of the benefactor, as did lavish use of gold leaf for ornaments and halos. And colour influenced composition too: an important figure in a narrative painting, or an important gesture would be coloured with a costly shade of paint by the artist, to draw the onlooker's eye to it.

Most striking of these expensive colours is ultramarine blue. Ultramarine is a pigment made by grinding the semi-precious oriental stone lapis lazuli and soaking the powder several times to draw off the colour. The first soaking produced the most intense violet-blue and was the most expensive. Graded use of ultramarines advertised the expense of a work of art. If the Virgin Mary's robe was painted with ultramarine of the quality of two florins to the ounce, then one florin to the ounce ultramarine might do for the robes of the saints who supported her, and this would also ensure that no mistake was made over who was the most important figure in the composition.

When Ghirlandaio was commissioned to paint an 'Adoration of the Magi' by the Prior of the Spedale degli Innocenti in Florence the contract which they both signed specified the materials and their quality meticulously:

'The blue must be ultramarine to the value of four florins the ounce; and [the artist] must have made and delivered complete the said panel within thirty months from today; and he shall receive as the price of the panel as here described . . . 115 florins.'

The painting was completed according to the terms of the contract, in 1488. The Virgin, her baby son perched on her knee cradled in the crook of her left arm, is indeed enveloped in the gorgeous folds of a vivid blue cloak of lapis-lazuli blue, thereby announcing the lavishness of the commission, and the prosperity of the foundation. At her feet, a prominent merchant donor kneels in worship, wearing as his badge of affluence a toning coat of deepest blue.

The Spedale degli Innocenti, where Ghirlandaio's 'Adoration of the Magi' still hangs today, is the oldest known charitable organisation devoted continuously to the welfare of children. It was founded by the members of the powerful Florentine Silk Guild, with a bequest of 1000 florins left by the wealthy merchant Francesco Datini, 'to increase the alms and devotions of those who have compassion for the boys and girls called "throwaways", so that these little children shall be well fed, educated and disciplined', and opened its doors to Florence's foundlings in 1445. Forty years later the Spedale had a staff of 25, caring for 171 vulnerable children. It still houses child welfare services today.

To the members of the Silk Guild who supported the staff and children of the Spedale financially, there was no contradiction in also spending lavishly on a building by Brunelleschi, and art by Ghirlandaio. By commissioning a magnificent building 'all'antica', with an elegant nine-arched loggia decorated with roundels by Luca della Robbia they would, they believed, be demonstrating to the world their wealth, civilised humaneness and generosity. Charity and genuine compassion could, for them, go hand in hand with expenditure on what some might regard as unnecessary ostentation. 'Alms and devotions' might be lavished on gifts and luxuries as well as on essentials for the poor.

At the heart of the consumer culture heralded in by the

European Renaissance there has always been a tension between generosity that is morally admirable, and decadent extravagance. As we enjoy the glittering Christmas lights and buzz of excitement in our high street, it is an issue with which we continue to grapple today.

Seven

At the beginning of December 2007, Belgium was plunged into political crisis by the absolute refusal of her French- and Flemish-speaking inhabitants to cooperate with one another in government. It made me wonder whether we might be entering an age of increasing national fragment-ation, and calls for independence by ever-smaller nation states.

Does size matter when it comes to nation states? Within the European Union, are ethnic or religious communities viable as 'nations', even if their economy cannot survive independently of its neighbours? These are questions Belgians are asking themselves at the moment with increasing urgency.

Belgium is in the throes of one of the biggest political

crises since it was established as an independent sovereign state in 1831. On December 1st, Yves Leterme, leader of the Flemish Christian Democrats, and the man charged since elections in June of this year with setting up a coalition government in Belgium, gave up trying to do so, and handed his resignation as potential Prime Minister to the Belgian king, Albert II. The king has given the outgoing first minister Guy Verhofstadt responsibility for brokering some kind of a resolution – so far entirely unsuccessfully. In the meantime he has interim extended powers to settle pressing political matters, like the country's 2008 budget.

The issue dividing the four main Belgian political parties is how much autonomy is to be given to the regions. The fear is that a disproportionate amount of power will be concentrated in the northern part of the country, Dutch-speaking Flanders. The French-speaking Walloons, and a smallish cohort of German-speakers, in the economically less prosperous south, are afraid that devolution will lead to Belgium breaking up along its linguistic faultlines, leaving the Walloons isolated and economically vulnerable.

Anyone who visits Belgium is quickly aware of the linguistic fracture that runs through the country. Dutch and French speakers watch different TV stations, read different newspapers, and attend different universities. Even the political parties divide into Dutch- and French-speaking. Leterme is a Christian Democrat, but the list of conditions he drew up for a coalition government was rejected outright by the French-speaking Christian Democrats. The very survival of the country is now in question.

When my graduate students change trains in Brussels on our way to our annual fieldtrip to the Plantin-Moretus printing museum in Antwerp, they are usually relieved to discover that Brussels is French-speaking. As we board the train for Antwerp (or 'Anvers' as it is marked on the Brussels departures board) I have to warn them not to try to communicate in French once we get there. Far better to speak English than to risk a tirade of nationalistic anger by accosting a Flemish-speaker in the tongue he associates with the Walloons.

These current tensions between Flanders and Wallonia as constituent parts of Belgium, have focused my mind on a matter that has arisen on a number of occasions since I began these *A Point of View* broadcasts. Regular listeners will know that I take their responses week by week (in the form of phone calls, emails and letters) rather seriously. On more than one occasion a listener has contributed something I had not thought of to my argument, or provided a correction.

But just occasionally emails and letters are, I have to say, quite intemperate. And no broadcast provokes a more indignant crop of responses than one in which I use the word 'English' rather than 'British' when talking about some feature of the history of the United Kingdom.

The matter has come up whenever I have spoken about a period in Britain's past before the Act of Union of 1707. When I referred to the early mariner and explorer in the reign of Queen Elizabeth I, Sir Humphrey Gilbert, as 'English', for instance, and when I described how, as his fellow-explorer Sir Henry Hudson embarked from St Katherine's Docks to sail the twelve miles down the Thames to Gravesend, from where he set out in search of the Northwest Passage, it was 'England' that dwindled into the distance behind him. 'British' and 'Britain' spluttered a chorus of correspondents. But no. As far as I'm concerned, I'm afraid not.

Even when Queen Elizabeth I was honoured with all her manifold titles and territorial claims, as in the dedication to Edmund Spenser's 1596 epic poem in English, *The Faerie Queene*, her titles ran as follows:

'To the most high, mightie and magnificent Empresse . . . Elizabeth by the grace of God Queene of England, Fraunce and Ireland and of Virginia, Defender of the Faith.'

To adopt the anachronistic 'Britain' and 'British' here, is, in my view, to confuse the historical record. We may be proud that such adventurers contributed historically to the prosperity and power of the country we know today as Britain, but we cannot require them to have belonged to a union before that union occurred. We might want to emphasise the extent to which tales from the pasts of Ireland, Scotland, Wales, and indeed those from more distant lands like India, Africa and the Caribbean islands are woven threads in the fabric of Britain's national story. But in context these narrative ingredients in the final mix need, I believe, to retain their original national integrity.

If we insist, we risk allowing nationalism to overwhelm truth. In the 1990s, Typhoo tea ran a television advertisement designed to play patriotically upon the intrinsic

'Britishness' of their brand of beverage. To accompany soaring aerial shots of the British coastline, green fields and breathtaking scenery, a sonorous, RADA-trained actor recited old John of Gaunt's emotive speech in praise of his country, threatened by factional strife, from the beginning of Act 2 of Shakespeare's *Richard II*:

> This royal throne of kings, this sceptred isle,
> This earth of majesty, this seat of Mars,
> . . .
> This happy breed of men, this little world,
> This precious stone set in the silver sea,
> . . .
> This blessed plot, this earth, this realm, this . . .

. . . the next word should, of course, be 'England'. But this was not apparently an option for the advertising agency that thought up the advertisement, nor indeed for Typhoo tea. Instead the quotation ended:

This blessed plot, this earth, this realm, this Britain.

I was not the only person, I feel sure, who experienced a frisson of genuine dismay at this unashamed misquoting of our national poet.

And yet – and here I return to the Belgian government's current impasse – my conviction that we ought to refer to Tudor England as just that, does not for one moment mean that I am in favour of dismantling the British Isles or the United Kingdom into its historically constituent parts.

For me, who lives where on the face of the globe, is not

much more than a historical snapshot. The location of communities in specific places and nations has almost always been the outcome of individual or mass migration, often enforced under pressure of politics or war.

In the mid-sixteenth century, the loose confederation of provinces and territories which make up the modern Netherlands and Belgium constituted one 'country', under Spanish occupation. When Catholic Spain, under Philip II, consolidated its hold over the southern Low Countries in the second half of the sixteenth century, and rebellion broke out in the North, Protestant Netherlanders fled northwards, to the protection of the Princes of Orange. Four hundred years later, Catholic, French-speaking Belgians remain largely concentrated south of Brussels, while Flemish-speaking Protestants predominate in the North.

Migration has also meant that many of those long settled in particular places, and whose loyalties and those of their families are firmly committed there, patently originate elsewhere. Today, once we get beyond the rhetoric of political parties, the idea that all those who live in Flanders think of themselves as 'Flemish' rather than Belgian, or those in Scotland as 'Scottish' before British, quickly dissolves into the natural diversity brought about by the constant movements of peoples. Whenever my close Scottish friend, who has lived in London since the 1980s and raised her two children there, tells me that 'eventually' she will go back to Scotland 'where she belongs', I ask her whether 'eventually' I am to go back to the Polish Shtetl my father's family left at the beginning of the twentieth century?

British I was born, and British I wish to remain. Not in any spirit of nationalistic fervour, but as a fully signed up member of the community of fair-minded individuals of every background, creed and ethnicity, who find themselves living, working and paying taxes in this 'green and pleasant land'. Though, come to think of it, in William Blake's rousing anthem, it is 'England's green and pleasant land', isn't it?

Eight

At an age when schoolfriends had photographs of Elvis Presley on their bedside table, mine boasted an old newspaper photograph – given to me, I suppose, by my father – of the handsome, sultry young Indian mathematician Srinivasa Ramanujan. Reading a novel based on his life, I wondered whether my early introduction to the wonders of numbers went some way towards explaining my life-long affection for mathematics.

I have been thinking recently about the way in which stories we are told when we are young shape our adult lives.

I am reading with great enjoyment a new novel entitled *The Indian Clerk*, by David Leavitt, based on the life of the early twentieth-century Indian mathematician Srinivasa

Ramanujan. I picked it up because I have such intense memories of my father telling me Ramanujan's story, at about the time I started secondary school, shortly after I had won a scholarship to a famous girls' school on the strength of my own mathematical promise. I even had a black-and-white photograph of Ramanujan, looking sultry and faintly like Elvis Presley, on the table at home at which I did my homework.

A humble clerk at the Port Trust in Madras, Ramanujan first came to the attention of European mathematicians in 1913, when he wrote a ten-page letter to the Cambridge mathematician and fellow of Trinity College, G. H. Hardy, which contained over 100 statements of theorems on infinite series and number theory.

Number theory is a fascinating field of mathematics. It consists of the study of the properties of whole numbers or integers. Among these, primes or prime numbers hold a special charm for number theorists, because of their peculiar power among the naturally occurring numbers.

A prime number is a number divisible only by itself and the number 1 (which is itself a prime, but for reasons I won't go into here is usually omitted from the list). The primes under 20 are 2, 3, 5, 7, 11, 13, 17 and 19. After that, primes occur increasingly far apart, sporadically and apparently unpredictably. For centuries, a great deal of mathematical effort has been expended on trying – unsuccessfully – to predict some patterned way in which large primes occur.

Let me try to give you something of the flavour of the

way in which prime numbers seem intriguing to someone with a passion for numbers in general. Take the number 2. 2 is the smallest prime number. It is also the unique prime which is even, because all even numbers are divisible by 2, and any number apart from 2 which is divisible by 2 is, by definition, not a prime. So mathematicians refer to 2, the only 'even' prime, as the 'oddest' prime.

Hardy was immediately intrigued by the extraordinary nature and complexity of the mathematics in Ramanujan's letter. But he was torn between believing that his correspondent was a crank, and wanting to recognise him as a natural mathematical genius. Having worked through some of the material in the letter with his fellow-mathematician and collaborator J. E. Littlewood, however, both men became convinced of Ramanujan's unusual ability, and, after some initial difficulties, Hardy contrived to get him to Cambridge.

There followed an extremely productive five-year collaboration between Ramanujan and Hardy. The two perfectly complemented one another's abilities: Hardy was a great exponent of rigour in analysis, while Ramanujan arrived at his results by what Hardy described as 'a process of mingled argument, intuition, and induction, of which he was entirely unable to give any coherent account'. Through his work in Cambridge, Ramanujan achieved the recognition he had sought when he first approached Hardy, and in 1918 he was elected a Fellow of the Royal Society (only the second Indian to be so honoured).

The British climate, however, took its toll on his health.

In 1917 he collapsed with a mysterious stomach complaint and was rushed into hospital, where doctors feared for his life. By late 1918 his health had slightly improved, and in 1919 he returned to India. But his health failed again, and he died the following year at the age of 32.

As a child, I found the whole story of the brilliant, self-taught Indian clerk who solved some of the most difficult problems in number theory and died so young, extremely romantic. But it was one specific anecdote about Ramanujan that particularly captivated me. It will be familiar to mathematicians, but it made a considerable impression on me at the age of 11.

Ramanujan was recovering from his first bout of serious illness in a nursing home in Putney, and Hardy had gone there by taxi to visit him. Hardy (never much of a conversationalist) greeted the sick man abruptly with the words: 'The number of the taxi-cab that brought me here was 1729. It seemed to me rather a dull number'. To which Ramanujan replied without hesitation: 'Not at all, Hardy! It is a very interesting number. It is the smallest number expressible as the sum of two cubes in two different ways.' 1729 can indeed be represented as $1^3 + 12^3$ and as $9^3 + 10^3$, and is the lowest integer for which such a combination is possible.

What intrigued me about the story, was that someone could have such a familiarity with the integers that he would spontaneously recognise an attribute of an apparently 'dull' or unprepossessing number as being susceptible of expression in a (for a mathematician) attractively patterned way. 'Every positive integer is one of Ramanujan's personal friends', was how Hardy's friend Littlewood described it.

Caring deeply about numbers and their properties may in part at least be something that runs in families. At the age of four, my daughter used to wake in terror from a recurrent nightmare: She was on a wide sandy beach at low tide. 'I had to count the grains of sand', she would tell me, tearfully, 'and I knew that I just wouldn't be able to do it'. Even at that age, numbers mattered to her intensely enough for her to dream about them.

But just as in some families, fear of spiders is passed on to the children who witness their parents' alarm at an arachnid in the bath tub, so terror of mathematics can be passed on from generation to generation. The role of good maths teachers in schools in encouraging pupils in this area, is particularly important, to overcome openly displayed anxiety on the part of parents about dealing with maths homework.

Last Monday the Royal Society published a 'state of the nation' report, on the UK's science and mathematics teaching workforce. The report concluded that there is a crisis in the provision of qualified specialist maths and science teachers in our schools, of which the government is largely unaware. This shortage is particularly alarming, the report goes on, because 'the skills, knowledge and understanding that come from learning and enjoying science and mathematics at school and college prepare young people for jobs in a demanding workplace and life in the modern world. With the guidance of a good teacher, these subjects become opportunities for young people to explore and wonder at the world around them.'

The shortage of well-qualified and committed teachers in maths has, I suggest, a particularly unfortunate effect in girls' schools, where it amplifies an existing inclination among many girls to insist that they simply do not like doing maths.

A London inner-city girls' secondary school of which I am a governor recently received a dazzling OFSTED report for its achievement across the board. The only area in which there was even a hint of criticism was in maths teaching at key stage 4. When a small group of us discussed the inspection report in detail with the Head Teacher, she was quick to explain that the problem was a rapid turnover in teachers and serious difficulty in recruiting well-qualified maths teachers at all.

But several people round the table inevitably also mentioned the likelihood that girls simply did not feel comfortable with maths, or even, could not do maths. It was not surprising, was it, if the school had difficulty getting all of them to succeed when it came to numbers and equations?

Thinking back to my own upbringing I feel sure that the problem lies elsewhere. All too often I watch my adult friends back away from a simple arithmetical calculation with the words 'I never could do maths'. This is not an excuse they would dream of making publicly with regard to reading. Perhaps, just as we try so hard to instill a love of great writers in successive generations, we should be looking for more stories like that of Ramanujan, to inspire all of our young people with a lasting love for the beauty of numbers.

...a little known story...

Nine

One of the things that gives me greatest pleasure about my weekly A Point of View *broadcasts is the emails and letters I receive, triggered by what I have had to say, which tell me fascinating (and usually highly relevant) things I did not know, or, simply had not thought of. Occasionally, too, listeners point out to me that I have got something wrong. Following my reflections on Ramanujan, a listener politely pointed out that I had been incorrect in saying that he was the first Fellow of the Royal Society of Indian descent (I have corrected the mistake in the preceding printed text.)*

Once again a listener has set me off on a productive train of thought. A small correction has prompted me to reflect on the way that we historians, in the very act of reaching out to recover the forgotten connections between ourselves and our forebears, run the risk of overlooking what is right under our noses.

But I begin with a little known story retrieved from the archives, that sheds some intriguing light on a piece of long-buried Elizabethan history. In the Beyazit Devlet Library in Istanbul is a document in Turkish, which contains an account of an exchange of gifts between the rulers of England and the Ottoman Empire in the 1590s:

'During the sultanate of Murad [it runs], the ruler of [England] was, it is said, a woman, Queen of a sizeable kingdom. This person, in order to approach the Abode of Majesty and the shadow of its protection, sent [sultan Murad] as a gift a masterpiece of craftsmanship, a clock.'

The so-called 'clock' was in fact a highly ornate clock-work organ, 'a work of art, studded with jewels', on which, according to the manuscript, the skilled technicians who accompanied the gift 'laboured for many years, toiling to complete and perfect it'. And although Queen Elizabeth I intended it for Murad III, by the time the organ had completed the long sea voyage from London in 1599, it was his son Mehmed III who received it enthusiastically, and had it assembled and tuned in the seraglio, for the entertainment of his harem. Captivated by the musical performance and the organ's whirling automata, Mehmed responded with lavish ceremonial gifts in the Turkish style.

Queen Elizabeth's and Mehmed's glamorous gifts to one another were part of a deliberate policy of cementing cordial relations between their countries. England and the Ottoman Empire had signed an agreement in 1581, granting English merchants preferential trading rights in the region, superior to any currently in existence with other European nations. Now, it was hoped that an Anglo-Turkish alliance might play a key role in creating an effective East–West force, to divide the military focus of the dominant and aggressively expansionist European power, Catholic Spain.

A generation later, however, the more austerely Islamic sultan Ahmed I had the clockwork organ destroyed. Nothing remains to tell us of its existence, except the documents in Turkish, Italian and English filed away in archives in London and Istanbul.

While this story is remarkable as a cordial sixteenth-century exchange between the Protestant West and Islamic East, it has a yet more unexpected sequel.

The musical mechanical marvel was not the only gift delivered to the court of Mehmed III. There was also a fine ceremonial coach, which was presented, with an accompanying personal letter from Queen Elizabeth herself, to the Sultan's mother, the Albanian-born Walide Safiye, who had enormous influence over the Sultan.

The Sultana was delighted. She wrote an effusive thank-you letter to Elizabeth in Turkish, in which she promised to use her best endeavours to ensure that her son stood by the treaty of cooperation he had signed with England: 'May you, too, always be firm in friendship! God willing, it will never fail.' Accompanying the letter was her own gift – a robe, a girdle, a sleeve, two gold-embroidered handkerchiefs, three towels, and a crown studded with pearls and rubies.

These were the formal communication and gifts, to go through official channels. But, delightfully, Walide Safiye sent a second, less formal letter, written in Italian on her behalf by her entrepreneurial 'Kira' or intermediary between the harem and the outside world, Esperanza Malchi, an Italian Jew – one of the English delegation described her as 'a short, fat trubkin'. 'On account of Your Majesty's being a woman', she wrote, the Sultana could without embarrassment ask a personal favour. Would the English Queen send her some English cosmetics, the renown of which had reached Istanbul:

'There are to be found in your kingdom rare distilled waters of every kind for the face and odiferous oils for the hands, Your Majesty would favour me by sending some of them by my hand for this most serene Queen; by my hand as, being articles for ladies, she does not wish them to pass through other hands.'

This long-distance relationship between an English Queen and a Turkish Sultana was short-lived. In 1600 there was a coup in Istanbul in the course of which Esperanza Malchi was murdered. Three years later England was ruled by a Scotsman, King James I. Nevertheless, this extraordinary sequence of documents – all of them to be found in the original and in contemporary Italian translations in the British Library in London – is evidence of contact and understanding between Eastern Islam and

Western Protestantism long before most people would expect.

Archival jewels like these Turkish letters have lain undiscovered for centuries in national and local libraries across Britain. No wonder the National Council on Archives – an organisation in Britain which exists to campaign for 'archives awareness' – maintains that the nation's collections of historical documents ultimately contain everything we could possibly want to know about ourselves.

In themselves, however, documents are effectively 'lost', unless they are reawakened by the attention and skill of an historian. It was only in the 1960s that the distinguished Ottomanist scholar Susan Skilliter brought the Turkish letters in the British Library to more general historical attention. And being one of those who can recover glimpses of the past from the glorious relics among the records carries with it responsibilities.

It was while I was working on this story that a courteous email arrived from Dr Rozina Visram, pointing out a piece of misremembering on my part in my last *A Point of View*. It made me rush off to the library of the Warburg Institute in London, to check that I had remembered the Ottoman Kira, Esperanza Malchi's letter correctly, and to retranscribe its detail.

Other alert listeners to last week's *A Point of View* will already have noticed the slip I made, in the course of telling the story of the Indian mathematician Ramanujan. I remarked in an aside that Ramanujan was the first Indian national to have been made a Fellow of the Royal Society.

And I wrote that sentence while sitting at my desk within the Royal Society's Library, with the entire resources of its almost 350 years of archives and records at my disposal.

Had I thought to check what I had, I believe, always been told, I would have found in a matter of minutes that Ramanujan was not the first but the second Indian national to become a Royal Society Fellow. The Parsi engineer Ardaseer Cursetjee from Bombay had been elected to a Fellowship almost eighty years earlier, on 27 May 1841. His nomination paper (lodged in the Royal Society archive) describes him as a 'Gentleman well versed in the theory and practice of Naval Architecture and devoted to scientific pursuits', and it credits him with having 'built a [sea-going] Vessel of sixty Tons to which he adapted a Steam Engine', introducing gas street lighting in Bombay, and 'having otherwise promoted Science and the useful arts in his own country'. He frequented the highest scientific circles on his visits to London, and on one of them he was presented to Queen Victoria.

The incident reminded me of the fragility of the jigsaw of human history we reassemble from its scattered documentary pieces. The sixteenth-century Ottoman Sultan's presents and letters belong to distant times and places. Recovering them requires all of our endeavours. Yet while we historians extend our efforts to try to give the past the depth and global reach needed to explain Britain's rich diversity today, our history closer to home may get forgotten.

Dr Visram assured me in her email that my error was

'not of much consequence, and does not in any way detract from what you were saying'. Perhaps so. But it is a timely reminder to those of us toiling in the archives that while we labour to recover the overlooked from the disparagement of history, we must also always take care not to be forgetful ourselves.

Ten

My Who's Who entry records that one of the things I like to do in my leisure time is cook. Which is especially fortunate as the Christmas season approaches each year, and I can take pleasure in preparing the dishes my family expects to see on the table for Christmas dinner. Just as importantly, it is the annual occasion for me to look out my favourite recipes for meals made with the Christmas dinner leftovers, to be eaten over the days that follow.

My year is drawing to a close in its all-too familiar way. As the season of New Year's resolutions approaches, what to eat and what not to eat are, as always, high on the agenda.

The annual debate in our family begins in the run-up

to Christmas, and is about the size of the turkey. As the chef, I favour a small, naturally-reared bird, and like to prepare it the way the French do, with a flavoursome chestnut, apple, salt pork and fresh herb stuffing, bound together with a couple of eggs.

The other members of my family want a huge turkey – like the one Scrooge sends to the Cratchit house at the end of Charles Dickens's *A Christmas Carol*. A turkey that, to Scrooge's delight, following his conversion to generosity, is so big that it 'never could have stood upon his legs, that bird. He would have snapped 'em short off in a minute, like sticks of sealing-wax', and which had to be dispatched in a cab because it was too big for the boy charged with the philanthropic errand to carry to Camden Town.

The enormous turkey is also a key part of the American Thanksgiving dinner we sometimes share with one of my sisters and her family in California – too big to fit in the oven, so, roasted over charcoal and hickory wood chips on an over-sized barbecue with a domed lid, and lovingly tended by my American brother-in-law, outside in the garden.

The issue at home, though, has practically nothing to do with the taste or style of the Christmas Day meal itself. What my family wants to be sure of, is that there will be lashings of leftovers.

I may insist that the slivers of truffle slipped carefully under the skin of my modest 10-lb bird give it a delicate flavour which complements the tart apple of the stuffing, but for my family what matters is that in the week after the Christmas meal there should be a whole series of occasions on which we get to consume what we failed to eat on the day. Cold turkey with leftover cranberry sauce on Boxing Day, and perhaps turkey sandwiches with copious quantities of pickle and mayonnaise the day after, followed by turkey pie, turkey casserole, and finally, turkey carcass soup. Leftover roast potatoes can be reheated in the oven too, and my husband is quite partial to refried brussels sprouts.

Under everyday circumstances I am keen on leftovers myself. I love to cook inventively, and find it a special challenge when I come home in the evening to find that the fridge contains nothing but the remains of the previous couple of days' meals, out of which I must create something tempting for supper. Turning the bits and pieces into a risotto or a hearty soup gives me enormous satisfaction, and a sense of being frugal.

The cookbooks of the 1960s and 70s were particularly good on recipes to use up what used to be called 'scraps'. Elizabeth David's *French Provincial Cooking* – first published in 1960, and my culinary bible when I was a graduate student – has a whole section headed 'Les Restes – The left-overs'. It recommends that left-over chicken and turkey be used in pilaff and in stuffing for paupiettes de veau, and I've successfully tried both. Today's cookery enthusiasts are more likely to turn to Nigella Lawson for inspiration. She too has a passion for leftovers, and I love the way she describes her own response to the leavings from the Christmas meal:

'To tell the truth, I'm happy to eat them standing, leaning on the still open refrigerator door, for my finger-picked breakfast, but I love the culinary fiddling to which they can lend themselves with great satisfaction.'

In recent years, however, something has begun to change where the housewifery of unconsumed food is concerned. Where once we were urged to clear our plates ('think of the poor starving children in Africa', my mother used to insist), now we are told it is good for us to stop eating as soon as we are no longer hungry. Just as not eating absolutely everything used to be a matter for moral reproach, now finishing up every last morsel of food is beginning to seem almost culpable.

We are enjoined by doctors and health advisors to chew slowly, stop eating as soon as we feel satisfied, and push the remainder of the meal to the side of our plate as part of today's conviction that otherwise we will all end up overweight. Being overweight, we are told, is the cause of practically everything that is currently a cause for concern in society, from burdening the NHS, to increasing the likelihood of getting cancer.

I remain an unreconstructed plate-clearer, and will continue to revel in what can be done with a few bits of cold meat and some yesterday's gravy. And my commitment to the ingenious use of leftovers involves a corollary. In order to have leftovers to be creative with, you have to have cooked a proper meal from first principles the previous day. There are only cold scraps where once there was something delicious and hot.

All over the country, especially in homes where both partners go out to work, the meals put on the family table have usually been purchased ready-made, the quantities perfectly judged for the modern appetite. There is nothing left over from meals such as these – indeed, we are told to discard the whole thing once it passes its sell-by date. And younger working singles or couples, shopping in their lunch-hours for such meals, have neither the time to prepare a dinner from raw, individually selected and purchased ingre-dients, nor the knowledge of cookery to do so. For many, Christmas is one of the few remaining occasions on which a meal is created from fresh ingredients, and consumed by the entire family, sitting around the festive table together.

A French friend of mine told me recently that at the Paris primary school her two small sons attend, serious cookery has been introduced into the curriculum for boys as well as girls. At a nearby restaurant, the chef and his staff instruct eight to ten-year-olds in how to prepare classic items from the French repertoire of cooking, and then how to present and serve them. At the end of term, the parents are invited to the restaurant, where one half of the class waits on them, while the other half cooks. Without such a conscious intervention, the school believes, the fine art of French cuisine will be entirely lost within another gener-ation. Cookery is, I suspect, a dying art in this country also, though it is no surprise that the food-loving French should have noticed before us.

I entirely understand that obesity is an increasingly prevalent medical problem that threatens to overwhelm the already over-burdened NHS, but advising us to leave meals unfinished is surely not an answer. Food waste is, in any case, already a recognised problem in Britain. Enormous amounts of packaged food we bring home from the supermarket get jettisoned without ever being eaten. According to a survey by the government watchdog WRAP, published earlier this year, we throw away a third of all the food we buy in supermarkets – that is more than three million tons of wasted food each year.

So, as usual my New Year's resolution this year will be to avoid chocolate and go regularly to the gym, to keep my weight strictly under control. I have generally managed to break that one by about the first week in February.

But this year I am also going to promise to resist the temptation of stopping off after work at one of the three convenient local late-opening supermarkets, to purchase a beautifully presented prepared meal, whose package graphics and accompanying text promise me a piece of culinary artistry, redolent with the fragrance of exotic faraway lands. Instead I resolve regularly to take the time to shop in advance, and cook from scratch, with real ingredients, selected with care from the increasingly attractive choice of fish and meat, vegetables and fruit in the local shops. So excuse me while I dash off to prepare that turkey soup my family is eagerly awaiting.

Eleven

The grand reopening of the Royal Institution in London, after a major refurbishment, in May 2008 – an occasion on which celebrity chef Heston Blumenthal made apple ice cream using liquid nitrogen, in front of the Queen – set me thinking about the glory days of science, when all of London's high society flocked to Faraday's scientific lectures.

Inside many of our historic buildings, spaces survive which seem to hold particularly strong memories of events that took place within them. One of my favourites is the Faraday Lecture Theatre at the Royal Institution in London, one of our oldest establishments dedicated to the promotion of science. Since shortly after the Institution's foundation in

1799, the world's greatest scientific communicators have stood in front of its baize-covered desk, at the centre of the steeply-raked 300-seat theatre to enthral the general public with their ideas and experiments.

What a contrast with today. Last week, Ofsted reported that at both primary and secondary school level, science lessons were dull and there were not enough practical experiments. Teachers no longer entertain classes with explosions of powdered magnesium; gone are the bunsen burners for heating noxious mixtures in fragile test-tubes: 'Science is a fascinating and exciting subject', said chief inspector Christine Gilbert, 'yet for many pupils, it lacks appeal because of the way that it is taught'.

It was in the Faraday Lecture Theatre, in June 1903, that French scientist Pierre Curie and his Polish wife Marie Skłodowska Curie demonstrated the remarkable properties of their newly discovered element, radium. The occasion was one of the Institution's celebrated Friday evening discourses, a fashionable event for which those who attended were expected to don full evening dress, and which caused such congestion on Piccadilly that Albermarle Street, on which the Institution stands, had to be designated the first one-way street in London, to cope with the crush of carriages.

The Curies were the scientific stars of the moment: everyone in London wanted to meet them. In the packed theatre, eminent scientists rubbed shoulders with leading members of London's high society, craning their necks in anticipation.

Actually, it was Pierre Curie who conducted the radium experiments, since propriety and the rules of the Royal Institution prevented a woman from participating in a Royal Institution discourse. Most of those present, however, understood that this research had been carried out by a perfectly-matched scientific partnership, whose complementary abilities were clearly evidenced by their many published papers. By 1903, the Curies had produced an impressive sequence of joint papers on the two new radioactive elements they had discovered – polonium and radium – but both Marie and Pierre had also published key results on the physics and chemistry of radioactivity independently.

At the end of that year, indeed, they were jointly awarded the Nobel Prize for Physics, 'in recognition of the extraordinary services they have rendered by their joint researches on the radiation phenomena discovered by Professor Henri Becquerel'. As a sign of the high regard in which she was held, Marie sat in the front row of the Faraday Lecture Theatre, alongside the most senior scientist present at that occasion, the former President of the Royal Society and towering figure in the investigation of electricity, Lord Kelvin.

In a partially darkened room, Pierre showed how radium emitted a ghostly light. He placed a piece of radium on a photographic plate which had been wrapped in thick layers of newspaper. Removing the paper, Pierre Curie revealed how the clear image of the radium had been transmitted through its wrappings, on to the plate. Finally, rolling up his sleeve, he showed a livid red area of damaged skin, where he had bound a sample of radium wrapped in a thin layer of rubber to his arm for ten hours. Marie, he explained, had suggested that this property of burning the skin might make radium a useful treatment for cancer.

As he moved his precious radium samples around, Pierre Curie's fingers fumbled badly. So incapacitated was he by his badly scarred hands and a general feeling of fatigue and debilitation, that he had not been able to tie his dress tie before the lecture. Neither he nor his wife was aware of the lasting damage being caused to their health by repeated handling of radioactive substances. Neither took any precautions when working at close quarters with radium.

So in this case, one of the 'lasting memories' I began with was a real one: years after Pierre's Royal Institution performance, it was found that the effects of his mishandling of his material still lingered on the premises – the lecture theatre had to be decontaminated, because of the dangerous level of radiation.

It is hard today to decide which attitude on that celebrated occasion was the more blinkered: the absolute inability publicly to recognise a great woman's scientific achievement, or the assembled company's unreserved celebration of, and unawareness of the dangers posed by radioactivity. For now, I'll stay with the former.

Among those in the admiring audience at the Curies' lecture was another distinguished woman scientist, the physicist Hertha Ayrton. A year earlier she had been the first woman proposed for candidature as a Fellow of the even more prestigious Royal Society, for her 'long series of experiments on direct [electrical] current arc, leading to many new facts and explanations'. After a flurry of activity on the part of the existing Fellows it was agreed that Hertha Ayrton's candidature was ineligible, because she was a married woman. Even had she been single, it was decided that 'the Statutes of the Society are framed on the footing that only men can be elected, and we think that no woman can be properly elected as a Fellow, without some alteration in the Statutes'.

Hertha Ayrton and Marie Curie – encouraged by the statutes of the Royal Institution to attend its lectures, but not allowed to take part in its serious business – became close friends. When, in 1909, the *Westminster Gazette* attributed the discovery of radium to Pierre Curie, it was Hertha who protested in a letter to the editor:

'Errors are notoriously hard to kill, but an error that ascribes to a man what was actually the work of a woman has more lives than a cat.'

But let's go back to all that messing about with dangerous substances – substances we now know could kill – for the entertainment of the public in the Faraday Lecture Theatre in the 1900s.

From the beginning, the Royal Institution was a place where science was both useful and fun. Its mission was declared to be: 'Teaching the application of Science to the common Purposes of Life'. And the public flocked to its scientific demonstrations throughout the nineteenth century. So why are so many people today happy to admit that they find science difficult and dull? Some of the blame may be laid at the doors of our education system, as the Ofsted report suggested. But there must be more to the flight from science.

People who would never admit to a lack of understanding of art or literature are happy to confess to total incomprehension where science is concerned. Yet our lives today depend as never before upon the outcomes of innovative science and technology. Without medical science, our lives would be shorter and more painful; without physics and chemistry, domestic conveniences that ease our everyday lives could never have been developed.

If, however, the reason for the general public's disenchantment with science is to be laid at the door of scientists unable or unprepared to communicate their subject so as to engage the interest and enthusiasm of non-specialists, then the Royal Institution is continuing a long tradition actively to counter such a trend.

It has just reopened after a major refurbishment of its original Albermarle Street premises by architect Terry Farrell – a refurbishment which thankfully leaves the Faraday Lecture Theatre improved but fundamentally unchanged, while transforming the rest of the buildings into an Aladdin's cave of enticing spaces fostering science education and communication. In her address to the distinguished audience of scientists and friends gathered at the official reopening, Director Susan Greenfield expressed the hope that evenings at the RI might once again be considered as thrilling a prospect as going to the cinema or out to dinner: 'You should be able to say "where shall we go tonight? I know, let's go to the Royal Institution"'.

And if you do decide to attend one of those captivating, cutting-edge Friday evening discourses, you can still enjoy arriving in evening dress, as you might for a night out at the opera. That is no longer mandatory – but it means that memories of the glory days of science still seem to hover over the Faraday Lecture Theatre.

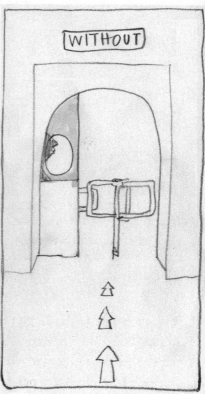

Twelve

As figures were released in summer 2008 which showed that the gap worldwide between rich and poor was wider than ever, I wondered whether, when the rich and powerful had so little understanding of how ordinary people live their lives, all of us are, in the end, equally disadvantaged.

The extremely rich are getting even richer. So we are told in the World Wealth Report, widely discussed in the newspapers over the past few weeks. The number of super-rich increased by almost 9 per cent last year. Last Monday it was announced that the annual income of the Prince of Wales has risen by £1 million, an increase of 7 per cent, very much in line with the general trend.

The wealth of the slightly less affluent – those who have

assets of more than $1 million not counting the homes they live in – increased even more steeply. In spite of the current 'credit crunch', nothing apparently makes it easier for you to make money than having a lot of it in the first place, and the rich currently have more to play with than ever before.

What do they spend it on? Private jets, customised yachts, fast cars and works of art; opulent homes with heliports on the roof, spacious cinemas, Olympic-size swimming pools and saunas, and kitchen facilities to allow them to call in the caterers whenever they fancy a cordon-bleu meal. With all these personalised and private possessions and amenities, they never ever have to rub shoulders nowadays with those less fortunate than themselves.

Which means, not only are the very rich getting ever richer, but they are also increasingly cut off from the common experience of those who are obliged to do things differently. Since they have no need to interact with less prosperous members of their community at all, they know increasingly little about us. They can if they choose turn their backs on the lives and circumstances of the rest of us.

It was not always that way. Last weekend I travelled back in time to a place where the worlds of those with lavish lifestyles were of necessity closely intertwined with those who provided them with all their everyday needs – the year was 1588, the place, Kentwell Hall in Suffolk.

Each summer for the past 30 years, Kentwell Hall has been transformed by owner Patrick Phillips and his wife

Judith into a living replica of itself in a given year during the sixteenth century. For three weeks continuously, between 200 and 400 volunteers, steeped in Tudor history, ranging in age from infants to sprightly octogenarians, live and breathe the period from dawn to dusk. Meanwhile, school groups and (at weekends) 'punters' like myself are allowed to wander around the house and grounds, watching them at work and eavesdropping on their activities. Like anthropologists observing a group of Trobriand islanders, though, we are asked not to intrude as the participants go about their daily business, and to accept that any question we ask will be answered from within the limited knowledge and understanding of somebody living over 400 years ago.

In the extensive grounds around the moated manor house, armies of artisans and purveyors of goods labour over the necessaries for the comfort of the Clopton family – gentry owners of Kentwell since 1385. The blacksmith at his anvil works iron, heated to red-hot in furnaces kept roaring by young apprentices manning the bellows, into horseshoes and tackle for the stables, and tongs and spits for the fire in the manor-house kitchen. At a treddle-operated lathe, a man with a chisel concentrates on turning a perfectly symmetrical wooden bowl for use at table. The bearded alchemist is bent over his still, transforming household wood-ash and distilled water into a caustic solution of lye – an essential ingredient, boiled with the imported olive oil and mixed with a little urine, in the fine soap used to wash the gentry's elaborate ruffs. Nearby one of his colleagues is keeping a watchful eye on a young boy pounding sulphur, charcoal and saltpetre together in a mortar, to make gunpowder for the gentlemen's wheel-lock guns and pistols (rumours of an imminent Spanish invasion are everywhere).

The attention to detail is, for an historian like myself, breathtaking. Labourers, gardeners and all kinds of artisans and pedlars carry out their work with meticulous care for its Tudor authenticity. Costumes are precise down to the last bum-roll under a gentlewoman's damask dress, and the exquisite black-work embroidery on her smock. In the dairy and bakery in the moat house, where modestly coifed young women with flour-covered aprons over their heavy woollen dresses churn butter and knead bread under the watchful eye of their seniors, the ambiance and atmosphere are so convincing that I could sit for hours, watching them going about their work.

All the Kentwell participants mingle and chat with one another for all the world as though they had never stepped out of the 1500s in their entire life. Leisurely conversations are conducted with passers-by, in convincingly authentic Tudor English. Right down to the smallest infant, everyone seems at ease with themselves and their community.

It is the great kitchen of the house that I return to for longest on every visit. There is little room here for onlookers, and one has to slip into any available corner to observe. Around the huge scrubbed table, cooks of all ages labour over food preparation that, without modern kitchen conveniences, requires dozens of pairs of hands to bring to perfection. Small boys fetch and carry, drag in logs for the fire, and take turns to rotate the spits. Pages and maids run hither and thither with ingredients and instructions, and then ferry the food in procession through long corridors to the waiting gentry at high table in the great hall. Tarts and pastries cool on window-ledges, delicious smells of roasting and baking waft around you, and everywhere magic worthy of Delia is being worked with long-forgotten Tudor recipes. There is a constant hubbub, an orderly chaos presided over by the formidable head cook.

In this bustle of people coming and going, fetching and carrying, it is simply impossible for the inhabitants of the manor house to forget those less fortunate than themselves. Nor can they, as they walk around the grounds, overlook the discomfort in which those who support their lifestyle, live and work. And the Tudor church saw to it that neighbours of all social degrees honoured their obligations to one another – there were rules for charitable giving to the poor, and rules of hospitality dictating that no stranger was turned away empty-handed from a householder's door.

Of course I'm being hopelessly nostalgic. The same Tudor community whose cohesiveness I am extolling was deeply suspicious of foreigners – including those who came from a neighbouring village – comfortable with allowing a man to beat his wife inside his own home, and pitiless towards vagrants or 'masterless men'. And if you were a child spit-turner, in that Tudor kitchen I so enjoy, working long hours for a pittance in the noise and the heat, it was probably not much comfort to know that the family in the parlour were aware that you were there, assiduously spit-turning.

But I suppose what I'm hankering after here is that sense of belonging – what is referred to in the typically lustreless terms favoured by politicians as 'social cohesion'. Last week was 'Who Do We Think We Are Week' – teachers and students in primary and secondary schools across Britain were encouraged to think about what it means to be British in terms of identity and diversity. The idea is that by encouraging students to understand and support each other, whatever their backgrounds or beliefs, we can create a more connected and tolerant society.

What my day at Kentwell persuaded me is that a sense of community has always been built on strong foundations of shared endeavour – doing things together, over long stretches of time. Mutual dependency creates a sense of responsibility – the knowledge that the good of the whole community rests on the shoulders of all those within it.

If increasing numbers of the wealthy never take public transport, never sit in a cinema audience or a doctor's surgery, or shop in the High Street during normal opening hours, that sense of the general good involving everyone is lost. The danger is, that confined within the CCTV-monitored walls of their palatial mansions, the rich stand apart from those ordinary kinds of social bond which bind communities together, so that they have absolutely no idea what it means – let alone what it feels like – to be poor.

Thirteen

Comments on the BBC magazine website following this Point of View of mine, in which I mused about the fact that many of the stories people cherish about great figures from the past have no basis in fact, turned out to bear out my argument entirely. Having taken as my example a story about Sir Christopher Wren's duping his critics by including redundant pillars in his design for the Sheldonian Theatre in Oxford, so many listeners and readers countered by telling me that the story really was true, but in fact referred to Windsor Guildhall (or Town Hall), that I was obliged to post a response on the BBC website pointing out that this latter building was not actually designed by Wren.

Never take a story at face value. That has to be the

watchword, for those of us whose job it is to paint a vivid picture of past events. Whether historians or journalists, we have a responsibility to sift through the stories we are told – even those recounted by eye-witnesses – collating them with the documentary and archival evidence, until we can be sure that the story is a sound one and its message reliable.

Ever since I published a biography of Sir Christopher Wren, the remarkable architect responsible for the rebuilding of London after the Great Fire of 1666, I have learned to anticipate a particular sort of contribution from some member of my audience whenever I have introduced Wren's name in a lecture.

The questioner will venture something like this: That was fascinating, but why did I not include the wonderful story of the pillars in the Sheldonian Theatre in Oxford – the building Wren designed to house the graduation ceremonies of the University just after the Restoration? It, surely, more than anything I had mentioned, captured the very essence of his virtuosity as an architect.

Confronted with Wren's ambitious plan to cover the grand interior space with a daring, unsupported ceiling, spanning 70 feet (so my interlocutor will continue), both Gilbert Sheldon, Archbishop of Canterbury, the patron funding the building, and the Oxford authorities demurred. Surely such a ceiling was unsafe and would be bound to collapse?

Under protest (he goes on), Wren agreed to add a run of columns, ostensibly to provide additional support. Years later, however, during renovation, it was discovered that he had left an air-gap of several inches between the tops of the columns and the ceiling. The columns did not support the ceiling at all, thereby proving to posterity that Wren's own original, interlocking-beam roof construction had been sound, and pillars were entirely unnecessary.

'That's a delightful story', I respond, 'and one I have indeed heard before. But what do you make of the fact that there are no columns of any kind – whether true or feigned – inside the Sheldonian Theatre?'

Nobody ever asked Wren to provide additional support for the Sheldonian ceiling. A team of experts was appointed to inspect it, in 1700 and again in 1720, because it appeared to be beginning to sag. That, however, turned out to be because the University had been overloading the ceiling from above, by storing books in the roof space. Once the 'great Weight of Books' had been removed, there was no further movement.

We still have the inspection team's second, 1720 report: 'We do hereby certify, that we did survey, and strictly examine the whole Fabrick of the Theatre, and do find that all the same is in perfect Repair and good Order'. 'We do further certify (they went on), That the Whole Fabrick of the said Theatre is, in our Opinion, like to remain and continue in such good Repair and Condition, for one hundred or two hundred Years yet to come'. They were absolutely right.

The story of the Sheldonian ceiling is so wonderfully evocative that it positively invites retelling. Eventually,

simple repetition convinces us that the tale must be underpinned by concrete evidence, and its trustworthiness
becomes established, in defiance of the evidence. It seems
almost a pity that a responsible historian has to point out
to the – often indignant – person who has told it, that it
has no basis in fact.

Beguiling stories of this kind ought not, however, to
blind us to more serious consequences of taking any story
of this kind on trust. It is troublingly easy to sentimental-
ise our tendency to be captivated by stories to the point
that we prefer the elegant nature of the tale to truth itself.
Nowadays, a plausible story – what journalists literally
call, 'a good story' – can gather momentum with stagger-
ing speed. If it is loosely based on known events and has
an element of truth about it, the public swallows it, and
fellow journalists then amplify it and embellish it. Such
stories can run and run, long after they have been discred-
ited as factually incorrect.

A responsible journalist has to exercise constant vigi-
lance against being seduced by a story-line – by checking
that the facts upon which the 'good story' is based have
been verified, sources examined and quotes meticulously
based on a written record. As a result, it turns out that the
very best and most conscientious of them are hard to
persuade that a story is true until they have run through
all those careful checks to their own satisfaction.

The veteran broadcast journalist Charles Wheeler, who
died last week at the age of 85, was famous for his scrupu-
lous reporting. Frequently putting stories together under

difficult circumstances, in sensitive war-zones, he was never prepared to base them upon anything but firm evidence. His searing story for *Newsnight* of Saddam Hussein's brutal quashing of the Kurdish uprising at the end of the first Gulf War is credited with having persuaded the Americans to set up the safe havens in Iraqi Kurdistan, which still operate today.

In 1952 Wheeler was the Berlin correspondent of the BBC's German language service, transmitting throughout occupied Germany. He worked for its nightly current affairs programme, aimed at listeners in the Soviet occupation zone. One of his contributors to a feature entitled 'Unsigned letters', came regularly from East Germany into the British sector of Berlin at some personal risk to take part in the programme.

One evening he dropped in to see Wheeler, expressing a desire to repay him for his many kindnesses. 'I've brought you a wedding present', he said, pulling a brown paper envelope from his jacket pocket. 'But I'm not getting married', responded Wheeler. 'Sooner or later you're bound to. Just open it'. He insisted that Wheeler accept his gift – 'Don't ask me to take the picture back. I've been through two checkpoints to get to West Berlin and if I'm searched on my way back home . . .' he added theatrically.

Inside the envelope was a painting on wood, a little larger than a postcard, of a woman in an elaborate high-collared dress, wearing a net of pearls in her hair and matching pearl necklace. Wheeler's colleague was extremely vague as to the painting's origins. He did hint darkly that he knew it to be extremely valuable. As to how he came by it – all he would say was that he had been given the portrait by a Red Army soldier in exchange for two sacks of potatoes to make vodka.

Charles Wheeler shrugged off the unverifiable story, and decided that the farmer was exaggerating the mystery surrounding the painting to impress him. No matter – he loved the little picture for itself. For more than fifty years he carried it with him on his travels, propping it up on his desk wherever he was based. He put the story of where it had come from, or how, out of his mind.

Then, in 2006 he embarked on a programme about the fate of works of art stolen during the Second World War, and showed his little portrait to the Chair of the Commission for Looted Art in Europe. Within weeks she had identified Wheeler's painting as a sixteenth-century original – a portrait of Eleanora of Toledo, the Spanish-born consort of the First Duke of Florence, Cosimo de' Medici, by an important court painter. It had disappeared from Berlin's Kaiser Friedrich Museum in 1944.

On 1 June 2006, in a small, discreet ceremony, Wheeler returned the painting to the museum in Berlin. It was, he said with satisfaction, a 'happy ending' to the story.

Charles Wheeler was, as we have heard from the many tributes over the past week, a reporter of integrity, a foreign correspondent in tireless pursuit of the truth. He was master of the events-based story, used to convey an important message to his readers or listeners. But he required any eye-witness story to be backed up with plenty of rock-hard evidence.

It gives me a very particular pleasure, as an admirer of Charles Wheeler's memorable reporting as a foreign correspondent over many decades, to remember that on this occasion, a story he had doubted and discarded as too far-fetched to be believed, turned out on further investigation – half a century later – to have been 'a good story' after all.

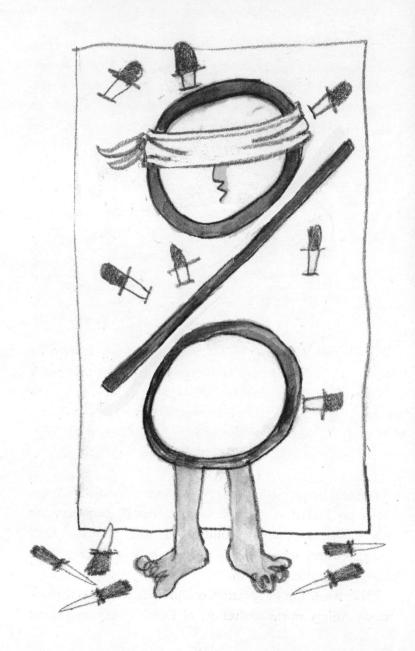

Fourteen

When a flood of new figures on knife crime was released at the beginning of July 2008, the government was quick to claim an overall decline in violent assaults over the previous period. Journalists grappling with the statistics seemed, however, entirely unable to agree on what they actually demonstrated.

As regular listeners will know, I am someone who has always been fascinated by numbers. So I find it disconcerting when those around me confess that they are filled with apprehension whenever they are asked to do a simple mathematical calculation.

This week the graduation ceremonies have taken place at my college in the University of London. My own small research centre runs a Masters in Research programme, and the marks accumulated by students from the various exercises and modules have to be collated and tabulated to work out their degree result. Since each module's mark represents a proportion of the sum total of those available, this involves calculating percentages – a task which seems to fill several of my otherwise highly competent members of staff with dismay, even though they are accustomed to processing arcane information from documents and archives.

Over the past couple of weeks we have been bombarded with figures by the media, on a range of topics, all apparently calculated to cause the person in the street the maximum amount of concern. Some of the stories based on these statistics have been the talking-point at practically every social gathering I have attended.

In the aftermath of what has felt like an avalanche of shocking news stories, multiple arrays of statistics have been produced, purporting to show a sudden, alarming rise in knife-related murders of school-age young people. These have whipped up public anxiety to near-panic levels with headlines proclaiming an 'epidemic of knife and gun crime', 'spiralling out of control', creating a level of youth disorder which adds up to a 'a national crisis'.

The first thing to say is that discrepancies in data-collection methods make it hard to get a coherent story out of these numbers, though the journalists have certainly tried hard. In spite of the statistics selectively used to fuel an alarmist story, all the available figures from reliable sources like the Home Office and the police, seem to be showing that incidences of knife crime have remained relatively steady over the past five years, while violent crime as a whole has actually declined. The 2007 British Crime Survey reported that '[the drop in violent crime] is part of a long-term trend – crime rates peaked in 1995, then fell by 42 per cent over the subsequent 10 years'.

A lengthy report by the Centre for Crime and Justice Studies on 'Guns, knives and street violence', published last month, summarises as follows: 'The evidence on knife crime contains a number of ambiguities, but combining the various data sets, a rather clearer picture emerges. Despite increased media attention, levels of knife crime have remained fairly stable at around 6–7 per cent of all violent crime.'

On the other hand, the concern that those involved in knife crime have got significantly younger does appear to be borne out by the statistics. Home Office figures obtained recently by a Liberal Democrat frontbencher show that the number of young people sentenced for possessing an offensive weapon in school rose from 15 to 90 a year between 1996 and 2006. And Department of Health statistics reveal that almost 14,000 people were treated in hospital for stab wounds last year, over 400 of them aged 14 and under.

According to the latest police figures, published this week, there were 22,000 serious offences involving knives in 2007–8. The 2008 British Crime Survey report reveals that over the same period 13 per cent of violent offenders were school-age or under.

The total number of knife murders committed a year has hovered around the 200 mark for years, and those most at risk are urban, male and under 25. Given the numbers-allergy I detect all around me, though, it is small wonder that the public at large is being swept along on a media-generated tide of fear. If so many people find simple numerical calculations hard to manage, how are they supposed to assess the data sensibly, or to recognise whether the sensational newspaper claims are correct? How can any of us decide on the basis of many column-inches of figures what our personal reaction should be, and how each of us ought to behave – or modify our behaviour – as a consequence?

Whether rising rapidly or holding steady, the numbers for knife crime are still small when compared to, say, deaths on the road. But for many it is enough that the threat feels real. As Cherie Blair said: 'Anecdotally it seems clear that the perception is that it's much worse'. Gordon Brown acknowledged last Monday that 'too many people, young and old, do not feel safe in the streets, and sometimes even in their homes, as a result of the behaviour of a minority'. Perceived danger has made many people desperately anxious – particularly for the safety of their children.

This brings me to the second set of tabulated numbers to have caught my eye this week. Figures produced by Halifax Financial Services reveal an unexpectedly sharp rise in private day school fees over the past five years. Fees have risen by 40 per cent, according to this report, which is double the national inflation rate over the same period.

The average annual private school fee is now around a third of gross annual average earnings. In 2003 it was a little over a quarter. In this case, on the evidence of those I spoke to this week, people are apparently more comfortable processing the numbers. They can do some very simple arithmetic to understand the costs of what is now happening. There is clearly a serious issue here to be faced by families who take the option of educating their children privately. If fees continue to rise at this rate, a child starting their private schooling this autumn could end up costing their parents £170,000 by the time they leave at 18, according to the Centre for the Economics of Education.

Figures like these might be expected to produce significant changes in patterns of education. Yet despite the increasing sacrifices that have to be made by parents, the number of children educated privately has gone up by almost 6 per cent between 2001 and 2006. Meanwhile, the number going to state schools has fallen. Parents who have chosen private education will, it seems, struggle determinedly with the fee increases, rather than move their children to the local comprehensive.

Faced with the lurid stories currently dominating our newspapers, of 11- to 16-year-olds with knives concealed in their school backpacks, is it any wonder that parents should be looking for any way they can to insulate their children from the threats of exposure to crime and intimidation on the streets and in the playground? The alarm generated by the banner-headlines about escalating knife-crime spills over into fear for our children in the classroom.

It is just such fear of what might happen in the next encounter, on the next street corner, that drives school-age boys to carry knives in the first place, according to Deputy Assistant Police Commissioner Alf Hitchcock, appointed by the Government to tackle the problem. Only 15 per cent of knife-carriers intend to take part in crime or gang activity. The other 85 per cent carry knives out of fear, in a world where they believe nobody else is there to protect them. In both cases, fear drives rational, responsible behaviour out of the frame.

The problems that underlie the apparent casual carrying and use of knives by young teenagers have deep roots. To begin to solve them, the debate has to be brought back from headline-grabbing expressions of moral panic and social despair, to a clear-headed and reasonable debate about long-term solutions. We need to sift and analyse the increasing volume of data that has been assembled on the where and why and how of violent crime, to arrive at a clearer picture of what is really going on.

Adolescent gang-members who carry and use knives, feel powerless, isolated and out of control. Responsible adults are not thus disadvantaged. They can, if they wish, take time to concentrate steadily on the facts before them, and to exercise their thinking and their influence to deal with the problem identified. But we have to master the data if we are to get to the root of that problem and find solutions. A good start to overcoming our irrational fear for our children on the city streets would be to begin by mastering our equally irrational fear of figures.

Fifteen

Throughout history the lure of diamonds – their exquisite beauty combined with their cost – has made them the gift of choice in all kinds of situations in which an exchange of precious items marks an important moment. The announcement that the internationally famous jewellers, Tiffany & Co., had been unsuccessful in claiming in the courts that the online auction company eBay had knowingly allowed counterfeit Tiffany pieces to be sold on its website led me to ask whether it really mattered if our gems were real or not.

The internet auctioneer eBay has won a significant battle in the war over the sale of luxury goods on its website. An American court has ruled that the internationally-famous jewellers, Tiffany & Co., failed to prove that eBay was responsible for the sale of fake Tiffany jewellery.

It had been alleged that eBay turned a blind eye to the sale of imitation brand-name jewellery, and that almost three quarters of so-called 'Tiffany' jewellery pieces bought on eBay were counterfeit. The court decided that it was up to the manufacturer to pursue those auctioning counterfeit versions of their goods.

One of the problems for high-profile brand names is, I imagine, that some of today's younger purchasers are quite comfortable with a Tiffany fake – particularly if it comes with plausible pale-blue packaging. High-street shopping has democratised dazzle: this week's must-have imitation designer earrings can be worn with panache, then discarded at the end of the season in favour of something new.

A ring or bracelet, however humble, can, of course, be given more lasting value by the memories associated with it. Today, friends or lovers exchanging personal gifts will still expect the stones in these to be real. The meaningful piece of jewellery *par excellence* is probably the diamond engagement ring – the modern version of which (a solitaire diamond in a six-prong setting, which raises the stone above the band for extra brilliance) Tiffany claim to have introduced in 1886.

The crowds queuing to see the new William and Judith Bollinger Jewellery Gallery at the V&A Museum in London provide confirmation if it were needed that it is the real thing that holds our interest. In well-lit cases, behind non-reflective glass, the visitor can get right up close to each of the over 3000 glittering gems on display. These cover the entire history of jewellery, beginning with a beaten gold Celtic breast ornament from the late bronze age, which arrests your attention as you enter the gallery.

One among many highlights is the Heneage or Armada jewel, presented by Queen Elizabeth I to Sir Thomas Heneage in the early 1590s. On its front is a gold profile relief of the queen, in a pearl-studded crown and ornate ruff, on a blue enamel ground, surrounded by an intricately worked frame of square-cut diamonds and rubies. Inside is an exquisite miniature portrait of Elizabeth by Nicholas Hilliard.

Then there are the nineteenth- and early twentieth-century high society necklaces and tiaras. In one of my early *A Point of View* talks, I reported that the Poltimore Tiara, worn by Princess Margaret at her wedding, had been sold at auction to a Chinese multi-millionaire, and I expressed the hope that British museums would court the new international rich to acquire and display such items. Shortly thereafter the V&A acquired the Manchester Tiara – a garland-style diadem made up of more than 1500 diamonds, commissioned from Cartier in 1903 by the Cuban-American socialite Consuelo, Duchess of Manchester. It now sparkles in pride of place in the new gallery, collecting a crowd around it.

Of course, the examples I have just given tell us that there is a fundamental difference between the gems in the Bollinger Gallery and the glittering ornaments with which women today deck themselves out on special occasions.

On the whole, only the fortunes of really costly, head-turning pieces of jewellery are recorded, as they pass from hand to hand, and generation to generation, thereby establishing a continuous narrative of acquisition and possession. It is provenance – the story of how particular pieces of jewellery have been lovingly kept and passed down – that provides precious stones with a history. As such, they can, like other material remains, form an important part of our understanding of the past.

Here, for example, is a telling story involving the provenance of a strategically stylish piece of jewellery, from my own recent research.

In March 1641, the Portuguese Jewish gem-dealer, Gaspar Duarte wrote from Antwerp to Sir Constantijn Huygens, First Secretary to the Dutch Stadholder – Holland's elected head of state, in The Hague. The letter informed Huygens that Duarte's son Jacob in London had located a particularly gorgeous piece of jewellery there – an elaborate, eye-catching brooch in the latest fashionable style, comprising four individual diamonds in a complicated setting, and designed to be worn on the bodice of a woman's dress.

Duarte was under instructions to find an impressive gift for the Stadholder's fourteen-year-old son Prince William of Orange to present to his bride-to-be, Charles I's nine-year-old daughter Princess Mary Stuart, on the occasion of their marriage in London that May. Because of the exceptional beauty of the design and setting, Duarte writes to Huygens, the four diamonds in combination have the impact of a single diamond of value 1 million florins – suitably impressive to be presented by a family of minor royals to the far more prestigious house of Stuart.

On 7 April, Duarte's son arrived in Antwerp with the jewel, and the following day Huygens examined it closely. But a fortnight later negotiations had stalled – the price proposed was, according to Duarte senior, nowhere near high enough. King Charles I had seen the brooch in London (he told Huygens) and offered a considerably higher sum for it.

The suggestion that the English King himself had expressed interest in the piece, was a shrewd way of applying commercial pressure, and was apparently successful. On 9 May, Duarte acknowledged receipt of payment of the asking price by Huygens on the Stadholder's behalf.

Shortly afterwards, the young Dutch prince, with an entourage of 250 people, arrived in England for his wedding, and was received at Whitehall Palace, where he presented members of the royal household with diamonds, pearls and other jewellery, to the value of several million pounds in modern money. The delightful van Dyck wedding portrait of the young couple, now in the Rijksmuseum in Amsterdam, shows little Princess Mary wearing her own diamond-studded gift, tied with a ribbon to the bodice of her exquisite silver dress.

When the English Civil War broke out less than a year later, Princess Mary and her mother Queen Henrietta Maria fled to the safety of William of Orange's court in The

Hague, and the jewelled brooch went with them. Thus within a year, this distinctive, exquisitely crafted, costly piece crossed the English Channel three times.

As a piece of dealing between London and the Netherlands here is an intriguing story of a luxury object which played a key part in a dynastic marriage – one which brought together the ruling houses of England and the Dutch United Provinces, preparing the way for the 'Glorious Revolution' of 1688, and eventually the Anglo-Dutch joint reign of another William and Mary. The wealthy Dutch Stadholder needed a gift which would impress the English King. The Duartes – suppliers of gems to Charles I in London – were close observers of English royal taste. The expert advisor to the Stadholder, Sir Constantijn Huygens, was fluent in English and moved freely between England and the United Provinces, rubbing shoulders with the aristocracy on his regular visits to the English and Dutch courts. The must-have appeal of the diamond brooch cemented relations between two ruling families, successfully straddling the geographical distance between them.

A story like this one suggests that Tiffany & Co. can stop worrying about the general availability of tawdry take-offs of their jewellery, offered for sale by unscrupulous vendors on the internet. In the end, it is the desire for the real thing that triumphs, producing objects of enduring beauty like those on display in the Bollinger Gallery. Most of us neither could, nor would wish to own such objects (personally, just the cost of keeping them safe would fill me with dread). But, the well-documented stories of their commissioning, who bought and wore them, who coveted and acquired them, together form a vital part of the historical record.

In some cases, indeed, posterity remembers individuals and whole family lines simply because of the name which attaches to a particularly striking heirloom, and the stories associated with it. After all, how many of us would remember the name of Sir Thomas Heneage, had his reward for provisioning the land troops in preparation for a Spanish invasion of 1588 not taken the form of the fabulous Armada jewel?

Sixteen

*Since antiquity, learning how to muster and present argu-
ments on either side of a tricky question has played a
prominent part in an orator's training for debating on the
public stage. But as evidence accumulates confirming that
it is human intervention which is accelerating global
warming, I wondered whether it was time to stop behaving
as if the arguments on both sides of this particular question
could be considered to be of equal weight.*

In a rapidly changing world, I am intrigued to find that
the ability to use Latin with confidence continues to provoke
widespread wonder and admiration. Last week, at the
opening of the exhibition on the Roman Emperor Hadrian
at the British Museum, the Mayor of London addressed

the assembled company in Latin, to general acclaim. Why, he asked the long-dead emperor rhetorically, had he failed to build in Britain a monument to match the Pantheon in Rome (whose remarkable dome Hadrian is supposed to have designed)? Instead, the Mayor continued, Hadrian's architectural legacy to us is something as humdrum as a wall.

Perhaps those who admire the Latin language are right. Heroic buildings are, as Boris Johnson observed, one of the Roman Empire's great legacies. But more lasting and far-reaching even than these is the influence of the Roman rhetorical tradition – an array of instructions and strategies for using language to persuade. Our legal system, public debating conventions, and even the way controversial topics are argued over daily in newspapers and on television, have all been shaped and defined by a method credited to the great Roman orator Cicero, and reduced to a set of practical rules in the *Oratorical Institutes* of the later pedagogic writer Quintilian.

At the heart of this system are techniques for arguing *in utramque partem* – being able to take either side on any contentious issue. The importance of 'argument on both sides' derives from the assumption that there are few debatable matters that can be settled simply by mustering the facts for and against. More usually, opinions on one side or the other of any argument are formed, and audiences swayed, on the basis of astute manipulation of limited evidence, backed up by an array of persuasive tactics, designed to construct a convincing case.

Quintilian calls such arguments *controversiae* – from which we get the word 'controversial'. In the Roman law courts this leads to a method of arguing forensically which is still known today as 'adversarial'. As these words suggest, arguing *in utramque partem* arouses strong feelings on both sides. Anticipating and controlling strong emotions is part of the training both Cicero and Quintilian advocate at an advanced stage in the training of anyone whose career requires a mastery of rhetoric in all its complexity.

As Cicero puts it, in his lastingly influential work 'On the perfect orator' (*De Oratore*): 'The man who can hold forth on every matter under debate in two contradictory ways of pleading, or can argue for and against every proposition that can be laid down – such a man is the true, the complete, and the only orator'.

So the great persuaders are those who can not only marshall the evidence on behalf of any question, but can also organise that material rhetorically, to present their case in the best possible light. And if called upon to do so, they can also present the opposite side of the argument just as convincingly. Except in cases of absolute certainty – where truth and falsehood are clear and incontrovertible – there is likely to be at least one accomplished advocate on either side of the question.

Roman discussions of exemplary forms of public debate are, I think, particularly relevant today. Our press and broadcast media currently thrive on the lurid presentation of controversy, particularly in the areas of science and medicine. Some of us are beginning to think that the tradition of adversarial argument is being tested to the limit.

Last week the media regulator Ofcom published its response to complaints brought against a Channel 4 programme shown in March 2007, entitled: 'The great global warming swindle'. The programme was written, directed and narrated by Martin Durkin – a film-maker with a reputation for being combative (he once made a programme which claimed that the medical dangers of silicone breast implants had been exaggerated for political reasons).

As the title makes clear, the thrust of the programme is that the formidable array of international scientists lined up in support of the view that global warming is caused by rising levels of carbon dioxide in the atmosphere, and that these rising levels are man-made, amounts to a conspiracy. As Durkin states: 'In this film it will be shown that the earth's climate is always changing, that there is nothing unusual about the current temperature and that the scientific evidence does not support the notion that climate is driven by carbon dioxide, man-made or otherwise. Everywhere you are told that man-made climate change is proved beyond doubt. But you are being told lies.'

This programme sits in an interesting way alongside another aired a year earlier – former Democratic Vice-President, and winner of the Nobel Peace Prize, Al Gore's 2006 full-length documentary, 'An Inconvenient Truth'. This presents with equally robust partisanship the case that a man-made global warming crisis is scientifically irrefutable, is indeed already upon us, and that action on the part of each of us is urgently needed.

Although Gore's programme is scrupulously argued and illustrated, it too has been challenged by those who disagree with its assumptions and conclusions. Last year a High Court Judge pronounced it 'one-sided', and found that it contained nine factual errors or exaggerations.

Ofcom received 265 complaints about 'The great global warming swindle' from individual members of the public, and a group complaint which included a number of eminent scientists. All were concerned that the programme was not presented with due impartiality and that it misrepresented the 'facts'.

In its judgment, Ofcom points out that it is not within its remit to pronounce on the accuracy of television documentaries. Only news programmes are apparently required by law to be factually accurate. In the time-honoured tradition of Cicero and Quintilian, TV documentary-makers are allowed to present their argument using any tactics and material they choose, as long as these do not willfully mislead.

In a polemical programme like 'The great global warming swindle', strong partiality is allowed in the interests of informed debate. Ofcom's view is that most people watching would be aware that there is a scientific consensus that human production of carbon dioxide is a major cause of global warming, and would understand that the views expressed in the programme are only espoused by a small minority. So, their ruling is that there was no harm in Martin

Durkin rhetorically tilting the scales of his argument in favour of that minority view.

On the other hand, the regulator said Channel 4 did break rules on impartiality. It also found that several interviewees, including the government's former chief scientific advisor, Sir David King, and Professor Carl Wunsch, of the Massachusetts Institute of Technology had been treated unfairly. In particular, they said, the programme had made some significant allegations without offering an opportunity for appropriate and timely response.

'An inconvenient truth' and 'The great global warming swindle' together provide an almost text book case for Cicero and Quintilian's *in utramque partem* debating. One might even propose that, on the evidence of the programmes, Al Gore and Martin Durkin are a good match for the Roman ideal of a 'perfect orator'. Each organizes his arguments and illustrative material with spectacular virtuosity. And judging by the widespread, heated debate both programmes have produced, the two spokesmen have gripped the imaginations of sympathizers and opponents alike. The resulting furore has succeeded in keeping the issue of global warming almost constantly in the public eye.

And yet the Ofcom ruling makes me profoundly uneasy. If, as the regulator maintains, there is a general consensus that we are ourselves responsible for increasing carbon emissions and global warming, then is it reasonable to use the format of the factual documentary to claim the contrary? If the case made in 'The great global warming swindle' is currently argued only by a small, vocal minority, then it is a distraction, taking up emotional time and energy. Meanwhile, the climate change clock is ticking. We need to stop talking about it and act now.

While believers and non-believers debate *in utramque partem*, we may already be headed towards global disaster. Personally, I don't want to take that risk. After all, look what happened to the Roman Empire.

Seventeen

In September 2008 I took up the position of KB Fellow at the Royal Library (Koninklijke Bibliotheek) in The Hague, where I spent happy days reading and transcribing the many hundreds of letters of the great seventeenth-century Dutch virtuoso Sir Constantijn Huygens (1596–1687). My frequent travels between London and the Netherlands during this period allowed me to indulge to the full my passion for travel by train.

Ever since my childhood I have particularly enjoyed travelling on trains. Trains give me a comforting feeling of independence and self-sufficiency, of being in control. From the station where you start your journey to your destination you know precisely in what direction you are going and how long it will take. You can make an excursion of it, choosing your route so that you admire the countryside and glimpse cathedral spires from your speeding train window.

On long journeys, you watch the landscape gradually unfolding, modulating from familiar to unfamiliar as you travel, and adjust your expectations while you are in transit. By contrast, a plane journey from a chilly, rain-soaked London to the South of France, tumbles you out onto the hot tarmac at Nice airport still wearing your waterproof shoes and heavy overcoat, and dazed by the easy Mediterranean pace of life after the hurly-burly of the city.

I have just returned from a research trip to the Nether-lands, to study an extraordinary collection of seventeenth-century letters in the Dutch Royal Library (the KB). The fellowship which enabled me to do this was awarded by the Netherlands Institute for Advanced Study, who provided my accommodation, half an hour away, idyllically situated in secluded woodlands, close to the sea and the dunes at Wassenaar. It was taken for granted that I would use public transport to get from the one to the other (the Dutch frown upon frivolous use of a car). So I travelled to and from the KB each day by train.

Dutch trains sum up the country's national characteris-tics – down-to-earth, sensible and conveying a comfortable sense of community and getting along together. My nearest station was in Voorschoten, 7 km from the Institute. Trains ran half-hourly from Voschotten to Den Haag Centraal, and sensible, sit-up-and-beg bicycles were available at the Institute to negotiate the network of broad, tree-lined cycle-paths across an endlessly flat, watery landscape to and from Voorschoten. On days when the rain turned from a drizzle to a downpour (and it does seem to rain a great deal in Holland) there was a free car park beside the station. The return fare to The Hague was under 4 euros, and the trains always arrived on time. Each morning I waited on the platform looking out over fields of grazing cows, marvelling at the ease and speed of my transition from rural calm to my desk in the library.

I am currently working on a Dutch seventeenth-century poet, musician, art connoisseur and diplomat, Sir Constantijn Huygens, whose long, eventful life spanned almost a century. As I made my way across the station concourse in The Hague, the destinations on the departure boards above my head evoked all the places Huygens frequented, from Voorburg where he built his elegantly classical country house, to more scattered locations – Leiden, Arnhem, Delft, Utrecht and Amsterdam. Names that recall Dutch paintings of the same period in which meticulously detailed skylines of houses and churches hover between wide blue-grey expanses of water and sky.

My daily journey also reminded me how taking the train keeps you connected to your fellow human beings. Everyone in Holland takes the train. You mingle with people from all kinds of background, and everyone seems to look out for one another – helping with heavy bags, offering information, or simply chatting about the weather. The well-to-do and the hard-up travel side by side. It takes no time at all to feel at home with the Dutch as a people when you travel amongst them by train.

My Dutch idyll was shattered the day before I was due to travel home. Naturally, I had come to the Netherlands by Eurostar and Thalys (the high-speed train that links Paris to Amsterdam). So imagine my dismay when I heard on the news that there was a serious fire in the Channel Tunnel and all trains were suspended. Within hours it was clear that there was no hope of the service being restored in time for my return journey.

Hastily, I booked a plane ticket from Schiphol airport to Gatwick. It all seemed so simple: check in online and print your boarding pass; hand in your bag at the desk marked 'bag drop' on arrival at the airport and there you are, ready to travel. As I boarded the train from Leiden to Schiphol, early on the Saturday morning, I began to wonder whether my attachment to this form of transport was sentimental – after all, my flight was scheduled to be not much more than an hour long, compared with the five hours it would have taken me with Eurostar.

Within minutes of entering the airport I had changed my mind. Schiphol is an airy modern airport, clearly signed to assist the traveller, and with ample encouragements to shop and enjoy yourself while awaiting your flight. But I am surely not alone in being enveloped by a pall of misery in airports. My bag duly dropped, I began following an apparently endless series of signs to the departure lounge. Almost at once I was brought up abruptly and without explanation in a long queue. Passport control (as it turned out to be) was unwelcoming, the immigration official unsmiling and suspicious.

Once past him, I continued to follow sign after sign, round corners, down long featureless corridors, up and down stairs towards my departure gate, with no clue as to how far I was going or how long it might take. It was twenty minutes away at a brisk walk. Having finally got there, there was the full array of security equipment to go through, manned by another set of unsmiling officials. Small wonder, then, that – unlike my train experience in Holland – passengers eyed each other warily, and nobody uttered a word. In fact, when, through force of habit, I ventured a remark to the person in front of me, I was brusquely rebuffed.

In such situations alienation sets in. We feel isolated and at risk, anxiously scanning the faces of our fellow passengers in case any looks strange or suspect. This is the feeling that makes many of us today nervous and afraid of the faceless 'masses' all around us, threatening our way of life.

I return to The Hague for another spell in the archives in November. Until I do so I want to hold on to that sense of belonging that using the Dutch local trains gave me. Because the feeling of sharing a way of life with all those who travel with you, and of recognising yourself as belonging to the large, diverse community thronging the platforms around you is, I believe, a vital part of our everyday lives. The experience of mingling and sharing is the social glue which holds us all together and tells us – there is no need to be afraid.

Fortunately, since I have been back in London, the experience of the past weeks has sensitised me to a comparable effect to be felt in the city in which I normally live and work. Each day the British newspapers are full of alarming stories about the breakdown of society – the chaos and danger outside our front door. But that is not how I feel as I travel to and from work. Now that I am back to my daily routine moving around London by bus and underground I can recognise how much this has in common with my Dutch trains. There too people of all sorts mingle and rub shoulders. Each improvement that is made to public transport, encouraging more of us to use it regularly, sustains and broadens that feeling of community I cherish.

Being surrounded by other people focussing on their own lives, brings moments of understanding like those I experience in the Netherlands: there is no hostile 'mob' – the masses – ranged against us, undermining our standards and values, roaming the streets, threatening us with their dumbed-down 'mass culture' and 'mass entertainment'. Rather what I see is other people like myself, reading, talking or looking around them. And just as often I feel I see them reflecting – facing surprisingly similar worries to mine: concerned about the speed of change, struggling to keep pace, hoping that we can explain all we are learning to the next generation. We are all, I recognise, 'the masses'. We are all in this together.

Eighteen

Towards the end of 2008 I was fortunate enough to attend the unveiling in Cambridge of the so-called 'Corpus clock' – a brilliant piece of inventive horology, built and financed by a man who had made his fortune from his part in another, more humdrum invention, the heat-sensitive bimetallic strip, which automatically turns off a kettle once it has boiled. I wondered why his name was less well-known to the general public than those of giants of pure science like Newton and Einstein.

The heroes of modern science preside like deities over our modern world. In spite of the alacrity with which so many people will announce that they are dunderheads where understanding science is concerned, almost all of us recognise the names of those who have made milestone scientific discoveries: Copernicus and Galileo, Newton and Leibniz, Darwin, Faraday and Einstein.

The names of those who have contributed inventions and engineered solutions to practical problems in our everyday world, on the other hand, are far less familiar and their names trip less easily off the tongue. We honour the men who framed the universal law of gravitation and proposed the general theory of relativity, but only a handful of inventors' names are instantly recognisable: Edison for the light-bulb, Dyson's vacuum-cleaner, perhaps. Few of us have any idea who invented the devices that make our lives easier: the transistor, the windscreen-wiper blade, the catseye, the sewing machine, the jet engine – to pick just a few we all rely on.

The eighteenth-century clock-maker John Harrison, for example, is hardly a household name. Harrison invented a mechanical clock precise enough to provide a solution to the problem of longitude. That problem preoccupied navigators until the arrival of Global Positioning Systems. Whereas a ship's latitude (its north/south position) is relatively easy to calculate as a distance above or below the equator, its east/west position is far more difficult. If a mariner knows the local time, and knows what the time is at the same moment at the zero meridian in Greenwich, then he can work out the angular distance travelled. But making such a calculation depends upon having a time-piece reliable enough to 'keep' the time set at the point of embarkation during the many thousands of miles and weeks the ship has travelled. Until Harrison came along, there was no clock that remained sufficiently accurate over long periods of time.

Harrison was a joiner's son from Yorkshire, with no formal education. Solving this problem consumed his whole adult life – spurred on by the offer of a handsome cash prize from the British Government to anyone who could do so. He devised a whole range of ways of counteracting the physical factors which prevent the clock's mechanism from running smoothly and behaving consistently. His very first clock, built out of a highly polished, oily hardwood, was virtually friction-free, eliminating one obvious source of error. He made complicated modifications to the suspension mechanisms, and created an elaborate bimetallic pendulum, to counteract the erratic movement of ships at sea, and the effect of temperature change on pendulum swing. He invented the so-called 'grasshopper escapement' – a brilliantly efficient mechanism for controlling the periodic movement of a clock's pendulum or balance wheel.

Eventually, in his seventies, Harrison produced a marine clock which satisfied the exacting requirements of the Longitude Committee, set up to judge whether any proposed solution fulfilled the conditions set for success in determining position at sea.

Much of the trouble John Harrison encountered in satisfying the Committee had to do with the opposition of one of those towering figures of theoretical science I mentioned earlier – Sir Isaac Newton – to all such (as he saw it) ad hoc solutions. Newton was altogether sceptical about any clock-based solution to the longitude problem. Clocks, he maintained, were merely useful instruments. Longitude had to be established using astronomical methods, specifically, the so-called 'lunar-distance method', which enabled a navigator to pinpoint his position based on extremely accurate tables of the regular movement of the moon. Characteristically, his submissions to the Longitude Committee as President of the Royal Society, concerning avenues to be explored in seeking a solution were irritable and uncompromising:

'I have told you oftener than once that the longitude is not to be found by clock-work alone. Nothing but Astronomy is sufficient for this purpose. But if you are unwilling to meddle with Astronomy, I am unwilling to meddle with any other method.'

It was only after Newton's death, and years of laborious toiling over the design and manufacture of his clocks that John Harrison was acknowledged to have provided a practical and practicable solution to the longitude problem, and finally earned the cash reward.

A week ago I was invited to attend the inauguration of a modern marvel of chronological invention which was officially dedicated to the memory of the largely forgotten John Harrison. On a bright, sunlit autumnal evening, a sizeable crowd gathered on the corner of King's Parade and Benet Street in Cambridge to watch Stephen Hawking – appropriately, our greatest living theoretical exponent of time – unveil the 'Corpus Clock', the brainchild of an Honorary Fellow of Corpus Christi College.

This extraordinary, entirely mechanical 'chronophage' or 'time-eater' has neither hands nor numerals to display the time. Instead, above a glittering 2-metre diameter gold-plated disk, a huge, jaw-snapping, rolling-eyed mechanical grasshopper rocks back and forth, apparently munching successive notches of the revolving dials with every passing second. Its movement triggers blue lights that dart across the clockface, registering the seconds and minutes as they pass. Each hour is signalled by a race of blue lights and the rattle of a chain dropping into an unseen coffin to remind passers-by of their mortality. Occasionally the pendulum hesitates to remind us that our perception of the march of time is subjective. Apart from its consider-able entertainment value, the clock's inventor said at the unveiling he 'wanted to make timekeeping interesting', by turning the clock inside out 'so you can see the seconds being eaten up' – literally by what is in fact a gigantic grass-hopper escapement.

Standing modestly to one side during last week's ceremony was the man who invented and executed the clock. Unlike the author of *A Brief History of Time*, I can almost guarantee listeners have never heard of him. Yet Dr John C Taylor was introduced to the onlookers as 'one of this country's greatest inventors', and so he is.

The rather considerable fortune which has enabled John Taylor not only to provide the £1 million the extraordinary clock eventually cost, but also the millions to turn the former bank building which houses it into a brand new undergraduate library for his old college (and I might add, educational bursaries including one held by a research student at my own institution) was accumulated as a result of a less sensational, more humdrum invention, but one which is now so ubiquitous that we all of us depend on it. It was he who perfected the kettle thermostat – the bimetallic strip which ensures that our kettle switches off once it has boiled merrily for a few seconds, rather than boiling dry. This simple, elegant little invention is used globally in a wide variety of thermostatically controlled domestic electrical appliances. It is hard to imagine how we would do without it. Why, then, does his name not figure on honours boards across the British Isles?

Clocks are only one among a roll-call of instruments and appliances perfected by technical wizards over the centuries. And as well as playing a vital part in all of our everyday lives, precision instruments like clocks are essential for testing the hypotheses of the very theoretical science which disparages the achievements of the inventors and technicians who designed and made them. No experimental science would be possible without clocks capable of measuring tiny increments of time.

Inventors like John Taylor turn the breakthroughs made by theoretical science into the applied benefits we see all around us – his company's website lists among their achievements not just corded and cordless kettles, but under-floor heating with a cordless connector, and a new coating to make kettles boil less noisily. Perhaps if our society were more ready to celebrate those who are ingenious, or 'good with their hands', and produce the inventions that allow us to lead comfortable daily lives, we would all become genuinely interested in the science that underpins the kettle and the clock. Perhaps more of our children would then decide to make science their specialist study at school and university.

But in order for that to happen, theoretical scientists in their laboratories and universities have themselves to be prepared to acknowledge the importance of engineers, inventors and technicians of all kinds, so that their achievements are celebrated as they deserve, and their names trip as easily off our tongues as those of Einstein and Newton.

Nineteen

The credit crisis of 2008 seemed to catch everyone by surprise – although looking back we can acknowledge it as having been almost an inevitability, given the banks' recklessness in extending credit to those who would never be able to repay their debts. As the crisis unfolded, there was a wave of general public disapproval of borrowing, lending and indebtedness. In October 2008 I reminded listeners that debt had played an important part in the rise of European culture.

As banks topple and stock markets plunge, it is hardly surprising that voices are raised blaming the current financial troubles on the evils of borrowing and lending. In an article in *The Spectator*, the Archbishop of Canterbury,

Dr Rowan Williams, expressed the view that the current credit crisis had exposed the 'basic unreality' of the long-standing global trade in debts, in which 'almost unimaginable wealth has been generated by equally unimaginable levels of fiction, paper transactions with no concrete outcome beyond profit for traders'. Those who make millions out of the financial misfortunes of others have, he said, to recognise and take moral responsibility for what they are doing.

It is an old point of view, and one with which many of us are inclined to sympathise. Christianity, like many other religions, has always frowned upon usury – lending money with interest – on the grounds that making money multiply itself, without labour or effort, is against the laws of nature.

During the European Renaissance, it was, nevertheless, financial measures almost exactly like those used by banks and financial institutions today which freed up the flow of wealth to produce economic growth, and thence the great flowering of art and culture, creating the accumulation of glorious artistic treasures now housed in museums and galleries worldwide.

In 1461, at the age of 17, Francesco Gonzaga was made a cardinal by Pope Pius II, as a political favour to his father Ludovico, the princely ruler of Mantua. Francesco had no particular aptitude as a churchman, but he did become a brilliant figure at the Papal Court, where he came to wield considerable power on behalf of his family.

The way he did this was by sheer ostentation – what in the period was referred to, with approval, as 'magnificence'.

A contemporary account of his first arrival in Rome describes how the size of his retinue and the sumptuousness of its trappings 'lifted the beholder's heart'. He entertained lavishly, and spent unstintingly on luxury objects of all kinds, which he displayed on public occasions, to underscore his wealth and power. The inventory of his worldly goods, taken for probate at his death in 1483, includes gems and intaglios, tapestries and hangings, damask 'turkish style' robes, velvet and brocade cushions, and silver and gold tableware.

Among Francesco Gonzaga's possessions, his collection of hundreds of antique cameos took pride of place. These were housed in a series of specially manufactured display trays, twenty of them of silver, embossed with the cardinal's coat of arms, two of jasper and one of green quartz. Widely admired by his contemporaries, the cameos also had the advantage of giving Cardinal Gonzaga access to a circle of other prominent collectors, including the Pope himself.

The catalogue of Cardinal Gonzaga's possessions, from his priceless gems to his exquisite manuscripts, makes breathtaking reading, but its opulent splendour is a dazzling illusion. To support his ostentatious lifestyle, the cardinal was in fact massively in debt, to the tune of something like 20,000 ducats – in today's terms a considerable fortune. At the time of his death, the cameos and their trays were lodged in the vaults of the Medici bank as pledges against what he owed – pawned to raise a loan of 3,500 ducats.

In spite of lengthy negotiations following Francesco's

death, these pawned treasures were never able to be redeemed. Their owner having technically defaulted on the loan, the cameos became the property of the cardinal's creditors. When Cardinal Gonzaga's family tried to retrieve them they were told they would have to find close to 5,000 ducats, because that was the value the head of the banking family, Lorenzo de' Medici, placed upon them. In the end they stayed in Medici ownership, adding to that family's own growing magnificence.

During the fifteenth century, merchants and bankers developed a variety of new financial arrangements which increased liquidity and allowed money to circulate freely. Bills of exchange became widespread – negotiable notes acknowledging receipts from the sale of goods abroad which could be cashed later at home in local currency at a profit. Bills of exchange could be endorsed by a third party, who took responsibility for the debt, and collected the added exchange value. In the sixteenth century, merchants began discounting bills, selling them to a third party before maturity for a smaller sum.

All of these strategies for the useful circulation of money depended upon confidence: trust in the wealthy merchants and bankers conducting the financial transactions, and confidence that the objects used as security against borrowing would hold their value. In the case of the cardinal's cameos, all the confidence-maintaining factors were well in place. The cardinal spent copiously on borrowed money, but the Medici bankers – soon to become princes on the strength of their immense wealth – were well-satisfied with the trays of cameos they acquired when he failed to repay his debts.

But on other occasions in the past, the financial edifice of credit and debt erected on a base of the high value of the commodity being traded, has proved illusory. A notorious historical example, familiar to many listeners, is that of the Dutch tulip.

In the mid-1630s the Dutch went wild about tulips. For a short period, starting in the summer of 1636, prices for the bulbs of particularly highly prized varieties rose to enormous heights. Tulip bulbs are of their nature objects on which it is possible to speculate financially. Those which promised to produce the most highly sought after, variegated red-and-yellow, purple-and-white or red-and white flowers — because they had produced such blooms in the past, or were the offsets from bulbs that had — could be bought and sold for extremely large sums. But the promise of the bloom lay resolutely in the future. What changed hands were a few brown bulbs the size of an onion. The purchaser had to pay upfront, and take the promise of a spectacular bloom on trust.

In early 1637 the bottom fell out of the tulip market. Speculative sellers who had bought at high prices to sell at a profit found themselves with worthless goods on their hands. Those who had purchased at the top of the market, and who would still see flowers as soon as the summer blooming season arrived, nevertheless refused to pay the balance on the exorbitant sums they had been foolish enough to agree to for their prize purchases in an overheated market.

Among those – from humble artisans to nobility – who had been caught up in the tulip craze, many were ruined, reduced to bankruptcy by investment beyond anything reasonable for a fashionable flower.

To serious-minded seventeenth-century men and women, the ephemeral bloom of the gorgeous tulip and the high price attached to it, symbolised the moral dilemma of conspicuous spending. If one accumulated wealth by legitimate means, was one entitled to 'squander' it on beautiful useless rarities like tulips, or indeed paintings and gems? Ought one not to dispense it more ethically, on good works, or invest it for the future? But the mistake the speculators had made was to overvalue their goods, and to 'bank on' (as we still say) their holding their value over time. Meanwhile, Dutch market gardeners had found a way to grow exotic tulips from seed, instead of relying on the expert splitting of bulbs, bringing the price of these still-covetable blooms down sharply.

Today, living as we do in turbulent times, we are, as throughout history, denied the luxury of knowing how future generations will look back on the present financial crisis. What we can be sure of is that the growth of sophisticated financial systems will continue to play an important role in fashioning the changes in all of our lives, including funding (often speculatively) the technologies that have transformed our world already from an agricultural to an industrial economy, and are now perhaps shaping the first post-industrial information economy.

Along the way many of us have benefited individually,

not least from the rise in personal home-ownership. So we all now have a stake in hoping that this present market correction we are living through turns out to have a gentle landing. We have to hope that, in the final reckoning, the homes we own, and whose values we have seen artificially soar over the past ten years or so, are like the cardinal's cameos and not a collection of perishable tulip bulbs.

Twenty

As an historian I know that what we call a 'family' has altered significantly over time, and that all kinds of combinations of people, related by blood or not, have been considered to be families and 'households' at different moments in the past. Yet they have all, in the end, shared a desire to have a secure roof over their head – a home of their own.

I asked in my last *A Point of View* whether, in the current mortgage crisis, our homes would, in the long run, hold their values. A number of those who responded – in letters and emails – were sure we had over-valued our desire to own a family home.

'An Englishman's home is his castle' was already a familiar platitude by 1700. To have a place of one's own for shelter, where dependents are protected and their posessions are safe, feels like a fundamental social good. But have we, perhaps today, gone too far in our quest for personal space and privacy?

The family as a unit has varied considerably in the course of history, but the bond between those who live under one roof together has always been an important one. Today, a 'family' tends to mean the tiny cluster of individuals related by birth – typically, father and mother and one or two small children, but increasingly, one adult and a partner or dependent – who share a residential unit. Until the nineteenth century, however, the word 'family' was a synonym for an entire 'household', and was used to cover all those who lived together in a dwelling, whether related by birth to the householder, employed in their service, or simply lodged with them. 'Home' was the bricks and mortar in which half a dozen or more adults lived their lives, supporting one another by their labour.

When the renowned humanist scholar Erasmus of Rotterdam settled in Basel in the 1520s, for example, his *familia* or family included a collection of friends, admirers and disciples, all living together in one comfortable, spacious house. Under the watchful eye of Erasmus's formidable housekeeper Margaret, these young men and boys – pupils, lodgers and colleagues – performed all the household duties their distinguished master required, preparing his meals, doing the housework, running errands and taking care of his horses.

Paintings of Erasmus like the one by Hans Holbein in the National Gallery in London show a solitary scholar in his study, surrounded by his books. But his was no isolated ivory tower. Even at work in his study on the Latin and Greek classics Erasmus had his *famuli* – his disciples, collaborators and factotums – around him. The same young men who staffed his kitchen and stable also worked as copyists transcribing from manuscripts, as scribes writing to his dictation, and as proof-readers and editors for his publications.

Throughout the seventeenth and eighteenth centuries, household-families like these were the standard type of group sharing a single roof. The historian Naomi Tadmor has argued that the family portrayed in Samuel Richardson's best-selling novel *Pamela: Or, Virtue Rewarded* (published in 1740) is typical of the times. Mr B – the squire who over the course of the novel's two volumes attempts unsuccessfully to seduce his household servant Pamela, eventually agreeing to marry her – is a bachelor, but nevertheless has a fully-fledged household supporting him and his lifestyle. These he refers to consistently as his family. As a waiting-maid, Pamela belongs to this community of domestic servants, distant relatives, friends and companions, all living in a single dwelling. She never refers to her 'poor but honest' elderly parents, who lived elsewhere, as 'family'. And the plot turns on the fact that she expects to be kept safe and protected within the household where she lives and works.

As family life moved increasing toward cities in the late-eighteenth and nineteenth centuries, houses of the type in which Mr B or Erasmus lived surrounded by dependents – big gabled mansions with plenty of nooks and crannies – continued to be built. But increasingly domestic structures centred on the housing needs of the growing middle classes. Scaled-down town-houses were put up, many of which still survive today, modified for modern use. These still provided lodgings for dependents and servants under a common roof, but centred on the family life of a group of blood-relations, in a way we can recognise.

Further down the social scale, accommodation was also always shared, but here it was fraught with difficulties. Just as happens today in rapidly urbanised economies, most of the working classes found themselves living in ad hoc ways, in overcrowded accommodation, which entirely lacked the privacy that we all now crave, and could hardly be said to offer the stable communal structures that Erasmus and Richardson wrote about. Social historian Amanda Vickery has recently explored in detail the way in which, in multiple-occupancy working-class homes in the eighteenth century, locked boxes, padlocks and keys to rooms and cupboards were talismans for hard-pressed lodgers, providing them with a remnant of private space and decency, away from the prying eyes of the landlady and their fellow-residents.

In our own times, the drive towards privacy has become paramount. We can see the modern ideal emerging in those wonderfully dated advertisements for domestic appliances from the 1950s and 60s, which show a smiling housewife, immaculately turned out in a many-petticoated dress with a cinched-in waist, pushing her vacuum-cleaner over expanses of carpet, or admiring her shiny new refrigerator. After the crowded, shared accommodation of the war years – shared washing and cooking facilities, wet laundry on the shared landing and a communal toilet – the domestic dream was resolutely a home with a front door of one's own. The promise of government to the returning armed forces was that social housing would make that dream a reality – would provide 'Homes Fit for Heroes'.

That dream is summed up in the so-called Parker Morris Standards, adopted for social housing in the 1960s. They became mandatory for council housing in 1969, and remained in force until 1980. The Parker Morris Standards laid down the dimensions for typical items of household furniture for which the dwelling designer should allow space, and provided anthropometric data needed to calculate the living space required to use and move around that furniture. Its rules specified that a 4 person terrace house should have 74.5 square metres of space; kitchens for 1 or 2 people should contain 1.7 cubic metres of enclosed storage space; in one, two and three bedroom dwellings the WC could be in the bathroom, but in 4 person houses it should have a separate compartment. The Parker Morris Standards for space, privacy and convenience continue to provide the familiar features of what we feel to be a modestly comfortable and convenient family home today.

But since the scramble for home ownership in the 1980s, our demands for personal space and privacy have come to dominate the planning and construction of domestic dwellings, and residential units have got ever smaller. Now is perhaps the time when we have to begin to ask ourselves whether the units of accommodation which have been constructed – often in glamorous high-rise blocks, with built-in appliances and fabulous views – are really, in the long run, fit for 'family' living, however we define that family.

In June of this year, at the launch of the London Festival of Architecture, the new mayor, Boris Johnson, deplored the fact that 'new buildings in London have some of the smallest rooms in Europe'. For new social housing to be provided in London, Johnson announced, 'we will be re-establishing the space standards first promoted by the visionary planner Sir Parker Morris'. The chair of the London Assembly's planning committee, Nicky Gavron, welcomed Mr Johnson's pledge: 'The mayor has been very clear that he thinks our space standards are shameful; that we are building rabbit hutches', she added. Others poured scorn on his promise, as an impossible dream – property values, they insisted, made reinstating the old housing standards out of the question.

We may have to wait until house prices have fallen dramatically before we know whether the homes designed for exaggeratedly 'nuclear' forms of living, offered by politicians and property speculators in an over-heated property market, were part of an impossible dream of home-ownership for every individual.

Perhaps the drive in Britain towards compact, separate 'homes', with ever-tinier floor-plans, crammed together by developers on restricted urban sites, is our housing equivalent of the Dutch tulip craze of the 1630s – our housing South Sea Bubble. If that bubble bursts, it is intriguing to imagine how these undersized dwellings might be combined and converted into homes for other types of *familia*, to suit the changing times, just as has happened so often in the past.

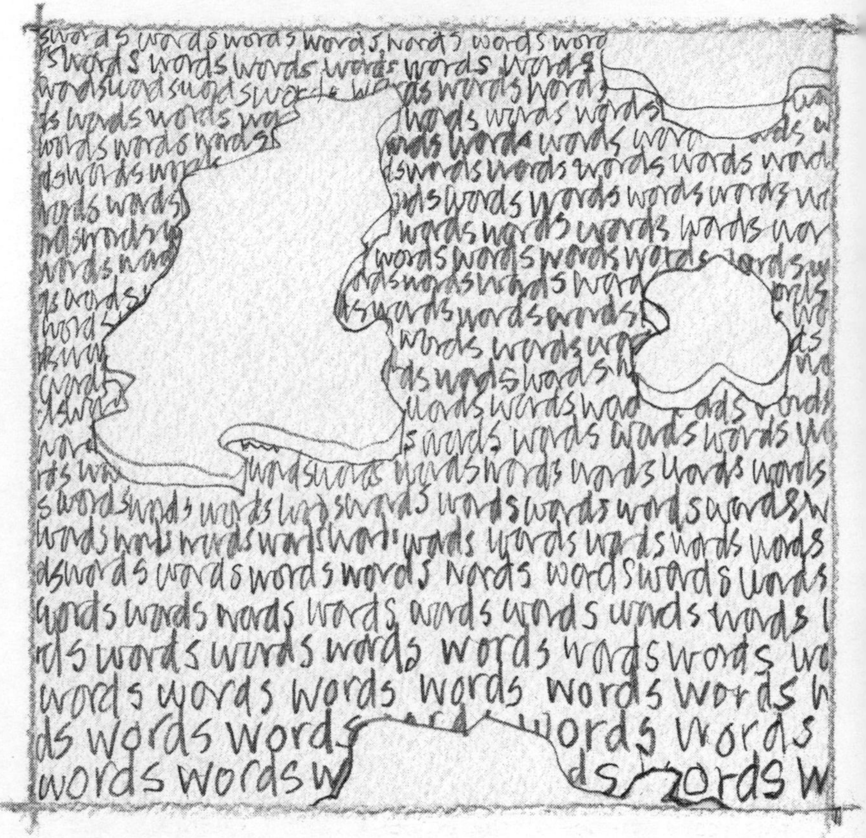

Twenty-one

When J. M. G. Le Clézio was announced as the 2008 winner of the Nobel Prize for Literature there was grumbling on all sides of the Anglophone press about the winner's literary 'obscurity'. I suggested that he was, in fact, a worthy recipient of this most prestigious of literary awards.

The announcement last week that J. M. G. Le Clézio is this year's winner of the Nobel Prize for Literature was greeted with a predictable chorus of indignation by the Anglophone media. 'Le Clézio: Who's he?' shouted the headline in the *Los Angeles Times*. 'I've never read his books. In fact, until Thursday morning, I'd never heard of him', confessed its columnist cheerfully, as he went on to deplore the way in which North American novelists have allegedly been consistently ignored and overlooked by the Nobel Prize Jury (the last American to win was Toni Morrison in 1993).

In the London *Evening Standard*, David Sexton was outraged at the thought that the Nobel Prize had gone to an author who is largely out of print in English. Le Clézio's work, Sexton had discovered, is barely available to non-French speakers: 'Why can't I read books by a Nobel Frenchman?' he complained. 'All I've been able to find so far, a few extracts from his most famous book, *Désert*, seem a bit simplistic about noble savagery. But what do I know?' Critic and literary commentator Mark Lawson revealed his own fruitless attempts to learn more about Le Clézio using an internet search engine: 'Inevitably, the choice of this Google-thin writer will revive accusations of obscurantism and pretension', he grumbled in the *Guardian*.

The Francophone press, naturally, saw it differently. As they were quick to point out, there is nothing obscure about Le Clézio's prolific literary oeuvre, indeed, he has been tipped to win the Nobel Prize for a number of years, and been the recipient of the most prestigious French literary prizes. French critics hail him as 'a great French monument who towers over our literature'.

Le Clézio was born in Nice in 1940, and raised and educated bilingually, in French and English. His father was an English government doctor, stationed in Nigeria. His mother was French, and both parents (in fact first cousins) were descended from a Breton family who had settled on the island of Mauritius in the eighteenth century. Mauritius is the setting for crucial episodes in a number of his novels – including his most recent work of fiction, *Ritournelle de la faim*, published this year – while he himself divides his time between Brittany and Albuquerque, New Mexico (where he teaches). Announcing the award, Horace Engdahl, Permanent Secretary of the Swedish Academy, described Le Clézio as 'a traveller, a citizen of the world, a nomad'.

Le Clézio's writing is nomadic too. His writing is a quest for understanding of the human condition, and it repeatedly takes the form of a literal journey. In *Onitsha*, the twelve-year-old hero, Fintan Allen, travels with his Italian mother on a slow boat to Africa. There the English father he has never known lives a faded colonial life, brutally exploitative of the local community, full of pettiness and posturing. Fintan meanwhile discovers Nigeria's disturbing energy and finds – in his loneliness and isolation – a kind of dangerous comfort in the habits and beliefs of the local population. This sense of comfort is disrupted when violence flairs, and the family are buffeted back to Europe to try once again to find their bearings. In *Révolutions*, it is the history of violent upheaval on the island of Mauritius that haunts the novel's hero, as he once again goes in search of himself and his family's origins on the other side of the ocean. Ricocheting between continents, the European fails to find settled contentment at either end of his travels.

'Exile and a search for a land to call one's own are the

very first things I was conscious of', says Le Clézio. 'It has always seemed to me, as Flannery O'Connor said, that a novelist ought to be driven to write about the earliest years of his life, when he first learned to understand the world.' The Nobel Prize Committee saw in him an Everyman – representative of no particular country or language – searching, like so many other migrants around the world, for some way to root themselves in an incomprehensibly shifting and changing world.

'He is not a particularly French writer if you look at him from a strictly cultural point of view', the Nobel Prize jury wrote of him. 'He has gone through many different phases of his development as a writer and has come to include other civilizations, other modes of living than the Western, in his writing.'

In fact, one might argue that Le Clézio is just the writer to honour at this particular moment in our European history. His novels capture with a painful acuteness the fate of the European, adrift in a vast unfamiliar world in which global social, economic and political realities impose themselves upon all-too-narrow national experiences. His protagonists wander anxiously, vainly looking for a reassuring, settled Paradise elsewhere – in Africa or South America – and finding instead the threatening unfamiliarity and violence of developing countries locked in their own struggles for independence. Looking for confirming identity, Le Clézio's itinerant heroes find themselves to be, in fact, irrelevant.

Le Clézio's novels also reflect the dawning realisation of

the west, in the week in which his prize was announced, that the fate of nations like Britain or the United States might be decided unexpectedly by the movement of a butterfly's wing on the other side of the world. How we understand ourselves is indeed dependent on what is happening in places we barely know. We have, perhaps for the first time, become painfully aware of the 24-hour operation of the global markets. We go to sleep to more or less comforting news from America, and wake up to find out how traders in Tokyo and Shanghai reacted while we slept.

Le Clézio's Nobel Prize was announced just as the public at large discovered – perhaps for the first time – that Iceland was to play a leading role in the unfolding financial drama in Britain. A volcanic island with a population of only 300,000, which had only recently shifted from relying on fisheries and agriculture, to becoming an international player in the field of financial services, this tiny Republic was suddenly in the spotlight because of the collapse of its banks. Only then did it become clear how many individuals in Britain had invested their life-savings in high-interest Icelandic accounts. Who would have dreamed that our financial destinies were inextricably linked to an unfamiliar land of mountains and glaciers, which many of us had only seen in television travel programmes?

Meanwhile, as the American Presidential Election campaign entered its final weeks, a report about the conduct of the Governor of Alaska turned the eyes of the world on this sparsely populated, remote state. Suddenly, a part of the world about which many of us knew little became the unfamiliar setting for a drama which could effect the political future of the entire world.

As Ivan Moore, an independent pollster based in Anchorage, Alaska put it, on the BBC Radio 4 *Today* programme on 11 October: 'Let's face it, before this happened people probably didn't know that Alaska was part of the United States . . . no one really knew who we were or what we were about. I mean, the fact that I'm sitting here in Anchorage talking to you guys, the fact that national people and international people are paying attention to what is going on in Alaska is extraordinary'.

We are gradually learning what it means to live in an information age, with the whole world on our doorstep at the click of a computer mouse. Our lives are no longer controlled by the decisions or autonomous actions of governments, separated from one another in individual nation states. National borders no longer provide protection from the movements of markets on the other side of the world. Our destinies depend on decisions taken in countries we have barely heard of, in the interests of and on behalf of people we may never meet.

J. M. G. Le Clézio's novels may only now have entered the wider European and American literary landscape, but his arrival on the scene as a world literary figure is extremely timely. As we struggle to understand who we are in this disorienting new global environment, the winner of the 2008 Nobel Prize for Literature is the writer to help us do so.

Twenty-two

The week in which I delivered this last A Point of View *was also a week of particularly discouraging news on mortgage defaulting and rapid escalation in personal debt. My editor at the BBC expressed concern over whether a broadcast on visible underwear might, under such circumstances, be considered inappropriate or insensitive. The following week, however, Marks & Spencer announced that in spite of a fall in profits in almost all areas of business, they had seen a sharp rise in underwear sales. Apparently, when times are hard and money short, luxury undergarments provide some kind of consolation.*

When I was at school, the whispered warning 'Charlie's dead' alerted a girl to the fact that her petticoat was showing under her lovat-green school skirt. Horror of horrors! From the age of eleven we all knew that our underwear ought never to be visible – a flash of white below the skirt-line was both an embarrassment, and potentially the occasion for a reprimand from a school prefect.

There are various theories as to where that curious phrase, 'Charlie's dead', came from. It seems to date from the Second World War, and my own favourite explanation is that in the 1940s, the window-blinds were lowered whenever there was a death in the house. The dipping half-slip below the skirt-line was like a lowered window-shade. More fanciful versions involving Bonny Prince Charlie or Charles II, are I am afraid, historically implausible, though no doubt a number of listeners will write or email me to say that they prefer them.

Until relatively recently, visible bra straps were treated as a sign that the wearer was, if not actually a fallen woman, at least someone who took insufficient care with her appearance – a likely symptom of slack behaviour in other areas of her life. A student of mine whose mother ran a fancy lingerie shop in Delhi once told me that her mother's customers were not prepared to buy silk camisoles with spaghetti straps because the maid who laundered them would consider them – and therefore their owner – scandalous.

There could hardly be more of a contrast with fashions in underwear, and acceptable attitudes towards its display in public, in the era of consumer affluence we have been living through, these past ten years. It has been a time for ostentatiously showing off surplus wealth. And one of the signs that a woman has money to spare has been for her to let beautiful, expensive items of underwear show. Lavish lingerie departments have blossomed in department stores across the country.

The impulse not to keep a prize purchase hidden from view has been reflected in the design of fashion too – from high street to haute couture. On the catwalks at this year's London Fashion Week, layering of diaphanous garments, with equally gorgeous underskirts and bodices, left nothing at all about the underwear beneath to the imagination.

This modern fashion trend, which seems to us to reflect our more easy-going attitudes to our bodies, is strikingly similar to the layering and glimpsing of undergarments of English sixteenth- and early seventeenth-century costume. This week sees the posthumous publication of the fourth volume in the great costume historian Janet Arnold's meticulously detailed series, *Patterns of Fashion*. Having documented every item of outer clothing for the period, Arnold has turned her attention to Tudor and Stuart underwear. The book is sumptuously illustrated with photographs of surviving items of the clothing our forebears wore next to the skin, including gorgeous detail of lavish embroidery, lace-work and stitching. And it shows clearly the ways in which men and women of substance also enjoyed letting their expensive underwear show.

Indeed, the most striking difference between underwear-flaunting then and now seems to have been that in Tudor times, it was not only women, but men too who adopted fashion designs which allowed them to reveal their under-garments. The process by which this gradual uncovering happened over time is fascinating.

The woman's smock and man's shirt, made of linen, were originally very similar garments – calf-length and long-sleeved, with a simple neck-opening. Worn next to the skin and washable, they protected the layers of finer fabric above from the wearer's sweat and dirt. Linen underwear offered a practical way of being hygienic while wearing outer garments of heavy expensive cloths, richly embroidered and adorned with jewels which could never safely be cleaned.

Over the shirt the man wore a structured doublet, over her smock the woman wore a bodice – or pair of bodies, as it was called then – with inserted strips of stiffening. The woman's layers of petticoats, underskirts and farthin-gales were attached to her bodice by 'points' (ornamental ties) drawn through purpose-made eyelets, as were a man's hose or leggings. These conjoined undergarments provided a base armature on which the sumptuous outer garments were displayed to produce an imposing, sharply-defined, tailored shape to the ensemble.

Over time, the shirts and smocks of the wealthy came to be made of finer and finer linen, and were decorated with increasing lavishness at neckline and cuff. The fashionable neck frill and gathered cuffs used more and more linen, so that special starching and setting were required to make them sit more tidily around the garment's neckline. They were eventually separated from the undershirt or smock entirely, for ease of washing and maintaining, and evolved further in decorative lavishness as garments in their own right. The neck frill grew oversized, into the elaborate, face-framing ruffs which for many of us define late Tudor dress, as it features in any number of formal portraits of royalty and nobility. Starching these became a laundry skill in its own right – the very first specialist ruff-launderer in England is supposed to have been a Flemish woman, Mistress Dingen Van der Passe, who brought Dutch-standard starching to London in 1564.

Detached ruffs and decorative cuffs were securely attached to the outer garments for each wearing, using metal pins. It has been suggested that in economic terms these pins are the first genuinely disposable commodities of emerging consumer culture, since they were bought in bulk, used once and then discarded (though there are records of the more frugal having their bent pins straightened for re-use).

Even without integral layered and embroidered neck-frills and cuffs, however, the amount of coloured embroidery on the upper part of shirt and smock continued to grow, transforming the simple undergarment into an object of beauty in its own right. At a workshop on Tudor underwear I attended last week, run by the Early Modern Dress and Textile Research Network, it was suggested that once these items of clothing were decorated with silver and gold thread-work – so that they became both uncomfortable next to the skin, and difficult to launder – another, simpler smock or shirt had to be worn beneath them, adding further to the layering.

As the shirt and smock grew more highly-decorated, ornamental openings were slashed in men's doublets and women's gowns to allow the wearer to show off the beauty of the embroidered blackwork on their underwear. Loose outer gowns, kirtles and waistcoats enabled women to offer revealing glimpses of the elegant structuring of their underwear corsetry.

I am sure there are those who mutter that recent flamboyant, underwear-exposing fashions are further evidence of a general decline in morals and decency. The close equivalence of fashions worn in the Tudor period suggests otherwise. The women who wore the extraordinarily smock- and undershirt-revealing styles of the late sixteenth century had to be seen as paragons of virtue by all. No well-born woman could risk being construed as provocative on the basis of what she wore.

Yet fashionable Tudor ladies were as beruffed and cuffed, and parading of their embroidered underwear as their male counterparts. Take a close look at any of the many familiar, exquisitely detailed portraits of Queen Elizabeth I, and you will quickly spot the heavily embroidered smock glimpsed beneath her bodice, the hints of lace at throat and wrist, betokening lace-edged and finely stitched needlework under her bejewelled gown.

What Tudor fashions share with more recent styles is the ostentatious display of garments on which the wearer has lavished significant sums of money. In both cases the expensive item is clearly a frippery – an unnecessary extravagance announcing that the person wearing it has extra cash to spend. I wonder whether, in the current financial climate, as frugality returns, it will once again become unseemly to display an elaborately embroidered bra, or show net petticoats under a twirling skirt?

The whispered warning 'Charlie's dead' dates from a previous age of austerity, after the Second World War. According to the Governor of the Bank of England, we stand poised once again on the brink of a recession. If things go as badly as the predictions of the gloomiest pundits suggest, will it soon be the case that women once again begin to alert one another to the danger of an immodest glimpse of petticoat?

About the Author

Lisa Jardine CBE is Centenary Professor of Renaissance Studies and Director of the Centre for Editing Lives and Letters at Queen Mary University of London, and is Chair of the Human Fertilisation and Embryology Authority. She is a Fellow of the Royal Historical Society and an Honorary Fellow of King's College, Cambridge and Jesus College, Cambridge. Lisa writes and reviews for all the major UK national newspapers and magazines and for the *Washington Post*. She presents *A Point of View* on BBC Radio 4 and appears regularly on arts, history and current affairs programmes for TV and radio. She judged the 1996 Whitbread Prize, the 1999 Guardian First Book Award, the 2000 Orwell Prize and was Chair of Judges for the 1997 Orange Prize and the 2002 Man Booker Prize.